THE FIRST DANCER

How to be the first among equals
and attract unlimited opportunities

"Eagles don't flock, you have to find them one at a time."

Ross Perot

The First Dancer

*How to be the first among equals
and attract unlimited opportunities*

By
MAJID KAZMI

Copyright © 2016 Majid Kazmi. All Rights Reserved.

No part of this publication may be reproduced or transmitted in any form or by any means, electronic, mechanical, or digital, including photocopying, recording, or otherwise, or by any information storage and retrieval system, without the prior written permission of the copyright holder.

Published by Valu Ventures Inc.
Ontario, Canada
www.valuventures.ca

Illustrations by Majid Kazmi
www.majidkazmi.com

Author photograph by Chris Dowswell Photography
www.chrisdowswell.com

Cover design by Maduranga Nuwan

ISBN-13: 978-0-9958-7421-3

This book should be cited as:

Kazmi, M. (2016) *The First Dancer: How to be the first among equals and attract unlimited opportunities.* 1st ed., Majid Kazmi

The advice and strategies found in this book may not be suitable for every situation. This work is sold with the understanding that the author is not responsible for the results accrued from use of the advice in this book.

ISBN-13: 978-0-9958-7420-6 (Hardcover ed.)

To all those who thought I would dedicate this book to them.

Contents

Preface   *ix*

Introduction   *xiii*

PART 1   The Success Mindset

The Basics of Self-empowerment: Victim vs Creator	19
Managing Self-expectations: The Pygmalion in Us	27
When Getting There Means Letting Go: My 4 Lessons	36
Attitudinal Leadership: It's Child's Play	43
Dealing with Rejection	48

PART 2   Reinventing Yourself

Personal Branding: Discover the Brand Called 'You'	57
Building an Attitude of Credibility	71
You Are Who You Know: My Experience With Networking	78
Know When to Keep Your Mouth Shut	93
Power of the Visual: We Hear With Our Eyes	101

PART 3   Being the First Dancer

The Law of Action: Your First Dance	108
Live to Give: Your Legacy Will Outlive Your Fame	117
Economic Freedom: Challenging the Norms	126
The Millionaire Mind: Thinking Rich	138

PART 4   What Lies Beyond

Happiness is Overrated: Learn to be Content   162
Wellbeing and the Nature of Work   170
Don't Let Success Come in the Way of Your Excellence   179
The Miracle in Your Head   191
Final Word   199

Acknowledgements   *203*
About the Author   *206*

Preface

A fourteen-hour flight across the Atlantic Ocean changed my life forever. On Tuesday, I was a senior executive at a bank; on Wednesday, a job seeker. I and my wife had taken a chance on a new country, and on everything we thought we possessed—our education, our talents and our optimism. We were past the point of no-return. We were so determined to make it work for ourselves and for our three-and-a-half year old daughter that we were gladly willing to sacrifice everything that had protected us thus far from the uncertainties of life—the things that constituted the status quo for us and kept us from considering taking any risks in life.

Arriving in Toronto on a frigid November night made us realize the enormity of the change we had embraced, perhaps unknowingly. Were we scared? Yes. Were we unsure? Yes. Were we demoralized? Hell, no. Our spirits were high and our ambition pumped a gushing river of hope into our hearts. Challenging our complacence made perfect sense to us.

Growing up, both I and my wife had a strong perspective on human purpose. We passionately believed in the higher reason for human existence than merely taking up space in the universe and traversing through time aimlessly. Having embraced this perspective since childhood helped us uncover our inner calling later in life; to use whatever potential we had to do something beyond what was expected of us most naturally.

For me, having a successful career was not enough if it didn't allow me to contribute at a higher level to the human society I was part of. In fact, being successful professionally was becoming more of a hindrance for me in reaching for higher goals in life. Still, I had been too afraid to give up my comfort zone—economically and socially—and to venture into an uncharted terrain. Moving half way across the world necessitated that I step out of that comfort zone and give up the privileges that came with being a successful banker. So with my family by my side, I took up the challenge. But things did not turn out quite as we hoped.

Over the next few months, I went through a struggle—both mental and physical—that was unknown to me. From financial challenges to a close encounter with death, I had seen it all. Few months later, when I sat down to reflect on my journey as an immigrant, I realized that I had gone through an incredible learning experience. I had learned a lot from my successes and even more from my failures. I had learned something new every day through the good times and through the hard times. Every person I met had taught me something knowingly or unknowingly, whether through kindness or through deceit. The truth is, I couldn't have learned in a lifetime what I learned in these four years.

But I did something more than that. I did not use my learning only to grow and accomplish more in life. I used it to grow others along the way. And it was the latter that opened up my eyes to a whole new world—a world of abundant opportunities.

Through this book I intend to do just that: share my learning with my readers and to open the same world of abundance to them. Through this book you will be inspired to dream and to act. You will learn the life lessons that take decades to internalize and benefit from. In this book, I have poured out my heart with just one intent—to inspire you to be the first dancer.

I didn't write this book because I am a writer, but because I had something worthwhile to say; because I had a story to tell. Over the past many years, I have delivered hundreds of talks on achieving success to people of all ages and all backgrounds. I have shared my real-life stories with thousands others through social media. Many in my audience encouraged me to share these stories and the lessons I took away from them with a larger group of people. They were convinced that what I had to say deserved a bigger platform. I did not see it possible except through a book.

This book is dedicated to the inescapable ability of the human spirit to be good and kind. It is dedicated to everyone who gives from what he or she has. This book is dedicated to all the first dancers it will inspire in the days to come.

Introduction

Who is the first dancer you might ask. How does it relate to being the first among equals and attracting unlimited opportunities? Or to begin with, why dance at all?

Good questions! First off, we all have unlimited opportunities for success. We can all benefit from the abundance that nature presents to us in the form of infinite love, infinite talent and infinite wisdom. The only factor keeping us from enjoying these opportunities is our ignorance towards them. We all look for opportunities in the form of an ideal state of affairs; the perfect weather for picnic, enough time to call a friend, or a good offer to sell the house. The truth is, *you* have the power to create the state of affairs that you call opportunities.

This book is directed to the common person—too busy to notice the abundance that engulfs him or her. Paradoxically, the first dancer is not an angelic enlightened soul, basking in the sun of timeless ancient wisdom. He is you, and he is me. He is each one of us. He is the common person negligent of the music that encapsulates his senses, too embarrassed to dance to the tune of abundance, lest he be called out.

The first dancer is the person who finally decides to let go of his false sense of possession and pride. He is the person who decides to be vulnerable in the face of uncertainties. He does not look for external opportunities or for benefactors anymore; he looks inwardly to what he possesses today. He reflects on the power of what the nature has already bestowed upon him. And he uses this reflection to make his first move. To the utter awe of the audience, the first dancer looks oblivious to the heckling of the crowd. He hears the music in his ears when no one does. He makes his moves when the time is not right, when the music is not loud enough and when no one is willing to dance with him.

The first dancer is comfortable being uncomfortable. He feels safe being vulnerable. He does not fear failure. His only fear is to miss the opportunity to dance to the tune of abundance and to let the music die out. In the midst of his indulgence, he attracts a certain subset of the audience—the few affable folks who actually feel entertained. The energy builds up slowly and pulls a larger crowd. Those who jeered at and disparaged the dancer now cheer for him. Lo and behold! In a few moments, the first dancer is joined by the second, and then the third. A movement is started. And the music is heard far and wide; not because it gets louder, but because the first dancer draws everyone's attention to it.

This book is directed at everyone who wishes to create opportunities out of thin air. It is for you if you are tired of waiting for the right time. This book is for you if you are bold enough to be the first dancer.

The First Dancer is divided into four parts; each comprising of small bite-sized chapters. These chapters are partly based on the articles I have written over the past four years and are a direct result of the life lessons I accumulated through my experience over many years. With the exception of chapters 6, 8 and 14, I have intentionally kept the chapters small so that you are not overwhelmed by the information presented on each topic and get quick breathers to digest it before moving on to the next chapter.

Part 1, *The Success Mindset* talks about the importance of creating a mental framework necessary to achieve success in life. This is the foundation upon which a life of accomplishments is built. This part of the book delves into the difference between victim and creator mindsets. It then looks into the dynamics of self-expectations and the role this intriguing phenomenon plays in positioning us for success. The following chapter examines how we can reassess what we think we have versus what we want; and how to let go of our sense of possession and entitlement—how to be vulnerable. The next chapter talks about the true nature of leadership. It looks at leadership not from the perspective of a position of authority but as an attitude that can be built into the human psyche and used to attract opportunities for success. The last chapter in this part presents ways to deal with rejection and to develop a mindset of resilience.

Part 2, *Reinventing Yourself* builds on the concepts presented in the preceding part and talks about the necessity of constant personal development as a means to position oneself to maximize the opportunities that might be presented from time to time. It focuses on the attitudes needed to become the first dancer. It includes chapters on personal branding, building credibility, networking, and communication—everything you need to know about standing out.

Part 3, *Being the First Dancer* focuses on the practical steps that lead to attracting unlimited opportunities. The chapters in this part are interlaced with the concepts of success mindset and attitudes presented in the preceding two parts. It examines the element of 'bias for action' that determines the opportunities for success. This part emphasizes the importance of being a giver in order to build a life of abundance. It presents practical tips on creating economic wealth by being the first dancer.

The last part, *What Lies Beyond* sums up the ideas shared in the first three parts and leaves you with some questions that you should ask yourself in order to attract unlimited opportunities. This part challenges you to ponder over what lies beyond opportunities for material success.

INTRODUCTION

The First Dancer is not one of the books that claim to provide a magical panacea to guarantee success in life by avoiding failure or fighting shy of change; on the contrary it establishes failure and change as the very basis for success. It only tells you how best to fail quickly. Also, it is not a step-by-step guide to achieve success, simply because having a "guide to achieve success" is an oxymoronic concept at best. It also doesn't present any shortcuts to getting rich, however it describes the change in mindset required to set you on path to financial independence.

Happy dancing!

PART 1
The Success Mindset

"Whether you think you can, or you think you can't—you're right"

—Henry Ford

Chapter 1

The Basics of Self-empowerment: Victim vs Creator

A young boy I was mentoring years ago as part of a program run by The Citizens Foundation in Pakistan blurted in middle of a group pep talk, "You don't understand sir, the whole world is against me; the teacher never gives me the marks that other students get for the same work."

Being a mentor, I was a bit taken aback by that downbeat remark but I realized that I had to be sensitive to how strong emotions from other students might come into play. Before I even had a chance to wrap my head around the possible nuances of the comment, another boy cut in "But sir, he does not even try."

Rewind one week to the orientation session; we all gathered in a small room already filled with a bunch of passionate boys and girls all wanting to make a real difference in the lives of less privileged students living on the outskirts of Karachi. An equally enthusiastic speaker adorned in crisp white shalwar kameez spoke about the Victim-Creator model of thinking. I was fascinated by how the speaker picked the best of David Emerald's The Empowerment Dynamic and Stephen Karpman's Drama Triangle and presented it in the most practical of terms. This learning had come to my rescue amid the impasse created by the boy's comment and his classmate's response.

THE VICTIM

The victim mentality is characterized by a person considering him or her a victim of others' actions. As a result, a victim is always complaining, criticizing and blaming people and situations—including things that are in his or her control.

Although it is a learned personality trait, in its basic form, it is based on the internal defence mechanism that all humans are pre-wired with. We have a built-in bias to select and interpret evidence validating the essential belief, "I'm okay." We all tend to look for external causes for our failures. Due to being hardwired with that essential belief, children are quick to learn this personality trait and get it ingrained in their psyche, making it a habitual behaviour.

The question is not whether there is actually an external cause of the pain and suffering that a person with victim mentality suffers. What matters is not what happens to them but what they do with it. The human soul is always looking to be at peace with itself. The way a victim seeks to achieve that peace is by blaming others for his or her sufferings and thereby sustaining the "I'm okay" belief. With time, this internal defence mechanism becomes an inalienable part of a person's character and used whenever the "I'm okay" belief seems to come under attack.

THE CREATOR

People with creator mindset go against the natural tendency that humans are born with. For them, their own behaviour is the cause of what happens to them. They are result-oriented; they look at the end-state and the big picture in any situation. For creators, problems take the form of challenges.

They understand the nature of problems and the role of others in creating them, but instead of considering themselves victims, they look inwardly for a way to solve the problems. They realize that problems will occur due to causes not in their control and that they will always have a choice. The choice they make is to adjust their behaviour to deal with what caused the problem, even if it is something external to them.

So rather than saying, "the problem occurred *due to your actions,*" a creator will think, "what is it that *I can do to influence your actions* to solve the problem." A creator will still be realistic in identifying the problem but will take a different approach to solving it.

THE CHOICE

Granted that we do not have a choice when it comes to other people's behaviours or things that happen outside of our realm of control, but we always have a choice of what we do with it in our minds.

The choice is simply this: do we want to relinquish the power of our own thoughts to others by letting them influence our thinking, and hence; actions, or do we want to empower ourselves and let only our own thoughts influence our actions. This basic choice underpins all human reactions to adversities. It makes the circumstance irrelevant and the nature of adversity not the only significant factor in your decision on how to react.

As human experience has shown, trying to achieve inner peace by blaming others and validating the essential belief is only an illusion. Accepting in our minds that others control our actions and the outcomes of those actions makes the inner peace unachievable in the long run. Victim mindset leads to depression, anxiety and learned helplessness, adversely affecting our behaviours and serving to reinforce the victim mindset.

By being consciously aware of this trap, our minds learn to raise an alarm every time we are falling prey to the victim mindset. As a result, we look for the best ways to respond to the challenge in order to minimize its negative effects or to even convert it into an opportunity. The solution to victim mindset is taking full responsibility for our actions and behaviours, regardless of the circumstances. When faced with a challenge, there is always something you can do, something you can change.

Since victimhood is contagious, it is important to be wary of situations and people that can lead you back to it. It takes a constant dose of reminders to truly believe that you have a choice. However justified you may think being a victim is, you have a choice to feel empowered and change the very situation that caused you to think of yourself as a victim.

Notwithstanding the rudimentary nature of this behavioural mechanism, I chose to explain the victim-creator model to the group of students to make them understand the inner workings of their young minds and to open their hearts to the world of empowerment. In retrospect, I am so glad I was able to convert some victims to creators.

* * *

Years later, after I had moved to Canada, a conversation with two gentlemen I had met for the first time reminded me of what I had learned with the kids at the mentorship program. I was looking for some inspiration to start a new life in a new country and any amount of motivation would have helped me get through the daunting settlement process.

A few weeks after we arrived in Toronto, we were invited to a dinner at a friend's place. When everyone had settled down in the living room, the host introduced me to the other guests; some of them, first generation immigrants. Among them were two men who interestingly had the same first name but looked quite different. We started with small talk. And as we began to have a conversation, I found out that they were both highly experienced chartered accountants. As if that wasn't surprising enough, I was told that they both acquired their CA designation in the same year and worked for seven years in the same country before migrating to Canada—in the same year.

As we touched on different topics, I realized that there was a remarkable difference in their outlook on life in general and career in particular. Despite having so much in common, they disagreed on almost everything from who will win the next World Cup of Hockey to which summer camp to send their kids to. As I began to feel entertained at their bickering and snuggled deeper in the cushy leather couch watching them amusedly as if they had come right out of a soap opera, I noticed a subtle difference between them.

One of them (let's call him Mr. Creator) sounded a lot more positive than his namesake, Mr. Victim. He looked like a good listener, he was eager to know other people's opinions and it seemed like he was genuinely looking to learn from others. Most of the time, he came across as solution-oriented and was keen on sharing his experience on everything from how he saved $5,000 on his new car to how he fixed the heating problem in his house. He seemed generally appreciative of whatever he had in life and sounded content.

On the other hand, Mr. Victim had a problem for every solution. At everything Mr. Creator would put forth as a potential solution, he would give a dismissive shrug and let out a small whine that always started with "but." On every topic, from economy to weather, he had tens of examples to show that things were not good and tens of people to blame for each of those things. Honestly, I agreed to much of what he said, but his constant griping became rather irritating after a while. The funniest thing was that he had no solution to offer on any of the topics discussed.

When the two men decided to have a heated political debate, I decided to intervene and change the topic. I was so intrigued at the difference in their mindsets, I wanted to explore it further. So referring to my own situation, I threw a question out to everyone in the living room, "What do you think is the best way to find work in Canada?"

Exactly as I expected, Mr. Victim volunteered first, "You will not find work in your field; no point trying." Before my facial muscles could flex to create an expression of "Err, what do you mean," he went on to narrate his own experience, "When I moved to Canada four years ago, I could immediately see that I would not be able to find work as an accountant." "The thing is," he added conclusively, "as soon as an immigrant steps into an office for a job interview, the person across the table has pretty much decided he is not the right candidate." My jaw dropped at that assertion and I saw a few people turning heads to look at each other.

As much as that statement perplexed me as a newcomer, I seriously doubted that could be the case. I knew that it was only a reflection of his own experience and perhaps a projection of his negative mindset. To test that hypothesis, I named a few employment agencies and bridging programs that I had heard of. I asked Mr. Victim if he had heard those names as well. His answer was 'no' to every one of them.

Since then I have forgotten much of what was discussed that night, but Mr. Victim's forgoing comment stuck with me for a while. I often used it as the perfect example to describe the difference between the victim and creator mindsets to my friends. Later, I found out that while Mr. Victim worked as a cashier at a gas station, Mr. Creator happened to be Director Finance at a manufacturing company.

For me it was quite an eye-opener. Despite having everything in common—same qualifications, similar work experience, living in the same neighbourhood, having spent the same number of years in the country, and even having the same first names—they were poles apart. No wonder one of them ended up being professionally and financially successful while the other took pleasure in demotivating strugglers like myself.

Remember that you have the same choice every step of the way. Whenever you are faced with the choice between looking at the bright side or the dark side, picking out problems in solutions or looking for blessings around you, embracing gratefulness or accepting thanklessness; you have to decide if you want to be Mr. Victim or Mr. Creator. This one choice will make the fundamental difference in what the universe offers you.

Chapter 2

Managing Self-expectations: The Pygmalion in Us

Let me admit. I have been meaning to write on the subject for several months. And each time I would put pen to paper; I would say to myself, "Wait a minute, I do not feel enough about the subject yet to come across as self-assured." It was as if something needed to happen to sweep me away in a whirlwind of undeniable conviction before I could say what I wanted to say since a long time. I wanted to speak as a practitioner and not as an academic.

J. Sterling Livingston's article *Pygmalion in Management*, originally published in Harvard Business Review in 1969 had struck me as undeniable truth, not for all the evidence provided but simply for the empirical nature of the assertion. It made perfect sense and helped me explain the mechanics of how expectations influence human behaviour—a phenomenon I had observed intriguingly as a student.

In Ovid's narrative poem "Metamorphoses," Pygmalion was a Cypriot sculptor who fell in love with a statue he had carved. Pygmalion made offerings at the altar of Aphrodite and quietly wished for a bride who would be "the living likeness of my ivory girl." Later he found that Aphrodite had granted his wish and he married the ivory sculpture changed to a woman under Aphrodite's blessing.

Despite years of credible scientific research on the subject, the spectacle continues to fascinate psychologists and experts in organizational behaviour and colossal amounts of effort to unravel the mystery persist to this day. To me however, my experience of a few weeks went one better than the years of scientific research at giving me the self-assurance I was searching for. This time around, an opposite experience proved the point.

Lucky enough for me, I was conscientiously aware of the phenomenon before it actually struck me. A senior leader, known for her caustic retorts and self-righteous conduct, much like for her flamboyant competence that intimidated coworkers rather than draw admiration or respect, had been picking on some team members for no obvious reason. She had been voicing concerns based on her feeling that a certain project would not be successful owing to the demanding nature of the undertaking and that members of the team (yours truly included) are unlikely to be successful at delivering the goods.

That feeling was so conspicuous and the message trickled down to the working team so frequently through multiple channels–both formal and informal–that we actually started believing that achieving success is a tall order. As some time went by, we got more and more convinced that our talents and abilities fell short of what was required to achieve the task at hand. After all, the feeling was being fed into our psyche by someone in a position of authority.

Sure enough, the project failed miserable. It went way over budget and could not even achieve half of the cost reduction target. This provided the leader with good justification for her prediction. As a result, everyone in the department started to believe that the team was simply not competent enough to complete the project successfully.

And then, one Saturday afternoon while I sat at a neighbourhood café, sipping my coffee and looking out the window at the birds picking straws from a sparse haystack, my attention was suddenly drawn to a mother telling her daughter that she was too young to do a certain chore. I turned my head to look at the four-year old's face as the glow of childish eagerness disappeared into a deluge of disappointment. I realized from her expression that she had clearly accepted her defeat even before taking a stab at the challenge. Notwithstanding my disappointment, it was an "aha" moment for me. Pygmalion was the first word that came to mind.

In terms of organizational behaviour, as much as high expectations of a leader serve to engender desired behaviour among followers, low expectations pull them down into a spiral of self-defeating reactions that have an adverse bearing on their behaviour and consequently, their performance. This is dubbed *The Golem Effect* to distinguish it from *The Pygmalion Effect*. The spiral would look something like this:

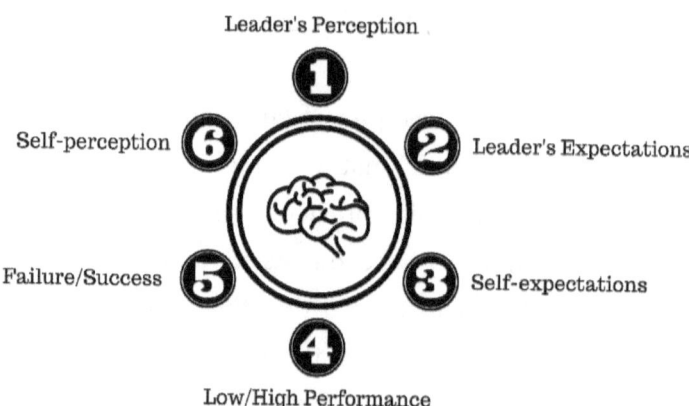

At the start of the spiral, the leader's perception of the employee would shape his or her expectation of the employee, which would affect the employee's self-expectation. The more positive the expectations are, the better are the performance and the result. This in turn would shape the employee's self-perception which would serve to reinforce the leader's perception of the employee.

Now remove the leader from this whole equation. Focus on yourself and your self-expectations. Just like the expectations others have of us play a role in shaping our self-perception and potential to achieve success, our own expectations of ourselves determine our potential and future success (or failure) to a large degree. It is a self-fulfilling prophesy of its own kind. Having started with negative self-perception, our ensuing failure further serves to cement our future expectations; again leading to a spiral of low performance and negative results, and hence more negative self-perception. While a person's self-perception is shaped by many other intrinsic and extrinsic factors and is seldom the first cause in this chain of cause and effect, changing the negative self-perception is often times the first step to break the vicious cycle illustrated below:

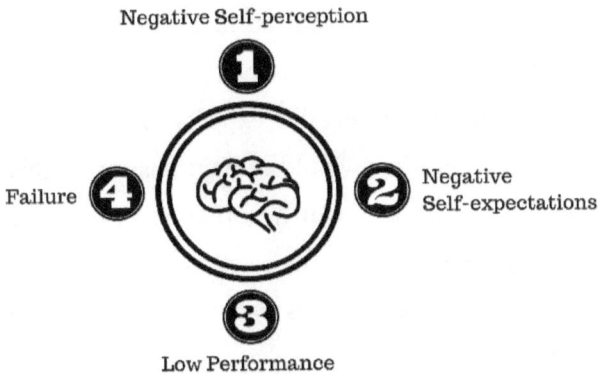

The CEO of one of the top global investment firms was asked the question, "What do you attribute your success to?" He responded by saying, "The more difficult people thought something was, the more determined I was to try my luck at it. So I treaded the paths where there was no competition. After some time, I was the only expert at things nobody ever had the nerve to do for the first time. And what gave me the courage to try out difficult things was my positive expectation of myself."

The younger we are, the more vulnerable we find ourselves to other people's negative expectations. This programs us to doubt ourselves. Later, we become our own enemies and don't depend on others for a generous supply of discouragement. In case of the little girl, the only way her confidence could have been shattered was by a negative expectation of an authority-figure; otherwise she virtually had no limits to her self-expectations.

In other words, by the time we are grown-up, our expectations of ourselves have already been shaped by others' expectations of us, much like a harness that would limit the growth of body parts. If in an ideal scenario, a child grows up insulated from the negative expectations of others around her, her self-expectations would remain positive, only adjusted from time to time by her own negative experiences. Therefore, the only negative effect to her self-perception would be by the reality of her experiences rather than by the perception of others.

The question then is, how to keep others' negative expectations from marring our self-perception and to keep the Pygmalion in us alive. Considering that mind is a receptacle of whatever is inculcated in it through the outer stimuli, creating a mental filter to others' negative expectations warrants building a higher state of consciousness that is more connected with the inner self than with the outer stimuli. The filter works to keep the negativity of the outer stimuli from staining the positivity of the inner self only when the consciousness remains submerged in the inner self. In simpler terms, it takes mental exercise to learn to shun the outer voices and concentrate on the voices of the uncorrupted inner self.

Conversely though, you would not like to ignore others' positive expectations that might shape your own positive self-perception. The key is then to selectively learn to ignore only the negative expectations and take the positive outer voices as a means to reinforce the inner positivity—positive self-perception and self-expectation.

Whether it is in an organizational setting or otherwise, being your own leader gives you the leeway to shape your expectations to suite you. That aligns outer expectations to inner expectations since the latter drives the former. The cycle starts from your positive self-perception and the spiral changes to:

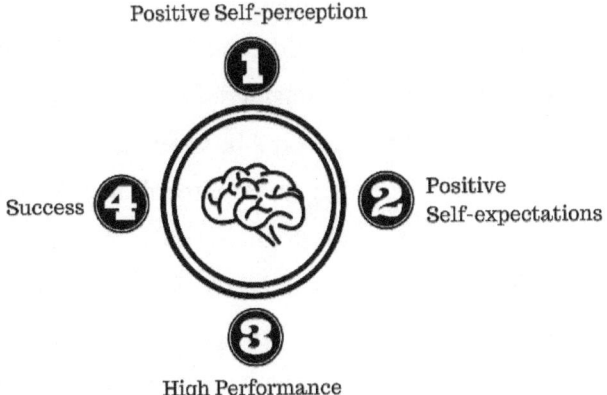

Switching from the formal spiral to the latter requires breaking away from the course to create a positive consciousness of the self. This can only emanate from within. If this is not done, a person would remain dependent on others' expectations for the controllable outcomes in his life; expectations that might not be positive at all times.

Considering the strength of the Pygmalion in us all, shifting the paradigm of expectation-performance relationship in the young generation can possibly raise the human potential to an unprecedented level. While this sounds daunting and demands a massive revamping of our educational, social, economic, familial, and political systems, we can always lead by example in our individual capacity by tapping into our inner conscience to create positive expectations of ourselves and our children.

As employers and leaders in our organizations, we must focus on increasing employee engagement in the decision making process to pass a positive message that the organization expects their expertise to add value to vital decisions. Employee engagement should be considered part of the organizations' cultural fabric and not merely a business strategy.

It is only through this approach to leadership that we can expect people to reach their true potential. Having high expectations of your team might not raise its potential in the short term but it surely will provide it the confidence needed to tap into its best abilities to come up to your expectations.

The first dancer is like a child in many ways; his self-perception not sullied by the expectations of others. He is aware of his true self-worth. His consciousness is connected to the inner self and serves as the filter for all external stimuli. Anything not aligned with his self-perception is filtered out and hence his self-expectation remains high, resulting in success when the self-fulfilling prophesy enigmatically works, much like Aphrodite's blessing.

The first dancer dances on.

Chapter 3

When Getting There Means Letting Go: My 4 Lessons

I was around nine years old. Hiding behind my desk in the classroom, trying hard to ignore my trembling legs and sweaty palms, I was dreading the imminent moment when the teacher would call out my name and I would have to come out of my snug invisibility cloak and be seen for all my limitations. This would be my first impromptu speech to an audience of more than one. Don't even ask me how it went.

As an impulse reaction to the experience I had been through, I decided to remain unknown. Comfortable in my anonymity, I had convinced myself that I had no interest in achieving success in life. I was in denial mode.

But there I was years later; reflecting on the experience that had shaken the very core of my self-esteem as a school boy. I looked inwardly in search of an explanation for my own behaviour. What I discovered was appalling. I was too afraid to let go of something I thought I had.

I didn't want to take the risk of doing the things necessary for making it to the top because I had successfully fooled myself into believing that I was already at the top. So rather than speaking up and coming across as unwise 50% of the time, I could just keep quiet and look intelligent 100% of the time. I needed to fool myself first to be able to fool others. And it made perfect sense to me. How can you lose the race when you don't take part in it?

I realized much later that the thing I was afraid of losing was something I never had in the first place. Hiding the real me behind my newfound self-perception, I hoped that others' perception of me would automatically align with it because that was the only persona they could see. My inaction could never let people around me know me, and not knowing me would mean not knowing my limitations. Oh, I remember how comforting it was!

LESSON 1: LET VULNERABILITY GIVE WAY TO STRENGTH

Today I know that my anecdote is not unique. Through what transpired in life in the years that followed, I learned that the only way to grow and achieve success was to expose myself to the world of uncertainty. The path of vulnerability was the only road to success. Not crossing over to that path every time I had the choice, diverted me further away from success.

It may sound paradoxical, but strength comes from vulnerability. You have to ask the question to get the answer, even though asking the question means you didn't know. Whatever your goal may be, you have to start from nothing to achieve something. Admitting that you have nothing is not a bad deal if that leads you to your goal.

So whether it is walking up to your manager and asking him what that popular acronym really stands for or wrapping your head around the new company strategy, get your answers and move on to the next questions.

LESSON 2: LOSE YOUR SENSE OF POSSESSION

Have you ever asked yourself the question, what is the real nature of the fear that keeps you from taking action? The most likely answer you'd get is that it is not the fear of failing to achieve something that bothers you; it is simply the fear of failing to retain what you already have—your wealth and material possessions, your fame and pride, your social status, family, work, recognition. It all emanates from our possessiveness and the list goes on.

As a general rule, to get from point A to point B you have to give up your present position and move towards your destination. Whether or not you'd be able to get to B is not known but you would know that only when you move away from point A. For career professionals looking to venture into entrepreneurship for instance, it is a scary thought to do what it takes to make the transition. You have to focus on your new business to make it successful in the future, but that would mean diverting attention from your job at present. What if you leave your job and finally make the transition only to wake up to the fact that your business is going belly up and would never amount to much. Too late to have your job back!

As dismal as it may seem at first, much depends on your definition of success and the intensity of your desire to achieve it. If owning a profitable business is your definition of success and your ultimate goal, you wouldn't consider yourself successful working for your employer. At some point in time, you have to give up your false sense of success to achieve what you really long for.

It is like a baby clenching her teddy bear while she sleeps. She likes to think that it is her mother she is cuddling and not a ball of yarn and fur. That gives her the comfort that knowing the truth never would. But with her hands full how can she cuddle her mother? Our self-perception of being wise and successful is really our teddy bear that we are too afraid to let go. Sooner or later, we have to let go of our false sense of possession to make way for success.

LESSON 3: IT'S NEVER TOO LATE TO CHANGE COURSE

We all make wrong decisions in life. Only because we have invested time, effort and money in those decisions, doesn't mean we cannot take the right decision anymore. I have seen seemingly happy couples breaking up after having spent decades together. I have seen bankers becoming successful artists, singers opening world renowned restaurants and doctors becoming acclaimed writers. They are all more satisfied with their choices and consider themselves more successful than before.

Of course you do not have to make an abrupt move. No matter how big your dream is, start small but take the first step now, even if it's as trifling as writing it down. Life is too short to keep mulling over your wrong decisions and keeping them close to your chest.

Besides, even after you have corrected course, you can still bank on what you learned from your wrong decisions. The banker-turned-artist can be great at managing his business finances. The restaurants owned by the singer should have the best entertainment in town. The writer who used to be a doctor can do a fantastic job of featuring doctors in her stories. In fact, they could all be more successful in their new careers than their competition if they transferred their knowledge from their past professions to their real passion; something others couldn't do.

LESSON 4: BEFRIEND YOUR FEARS

Fear is second nature to us. We are afraid of everything from the unpredictability of the weather to financial instability and career choices. There is no shame in admitting that.

In fact, we ought to be aware of our fears so that we could use them to our advantage. Yes, that's right; our fears can be the stepping stones to our personal development and success.

Deep inside us all, there is a perpetual conflict between our urge to succeed and the fear of taking action. The trouble is, taking action almost always precedes success. For the successful among us, fear is the best friend; advising us what actions to take, especially when it comes to difficult choices in life.

Sometimes our ambition to progress in life and our fear of failure come face to face. Sometimes we feel like getting out of bed in the morning and staying curled up at the same time. We want to stay at home and go out with friends, work on our million-dollar business plan or just chill out, have the world know us and stay on being anonymous—all at the same moment. These are all cues to tell us that there is an inner tumult arising out of a conflict between the forces of fear and ambition somewhere deep inside us. Because one of the two forces has to win the tug of war, our odds of success are 50/50 at this stage.

So by default we are all complacent with the status-quo, not too keen to push ourselves to accept challenges in life. Something has to happen within us to change this feeling and let the force of ambition win the fight against fear so that we improve our odds of success. Being aware of the cues can help us identify when exactly we need to take action and shift the fear-ambition balance to our advantage.

Know deep in your heart that the things you are most afraid of are precisely the things that will lead you to success in life. Whether it is your next live gig, walking up to someone and saying hi, applying for the next job or pitching your business idea, every time you come across fear, pierce right through it and take a stab at that very thing that shakes you like a leaf. That is the only way to let go of your false pride and your crippling complacence.

All four lessons above would make sense only when you have a clear goal in sight. Letting go works only when you are truly passionate about what you want to achieve in life. Again, starting small and acting now is the key that cannot be overemphasized.

The first dancer's ambition to be known is greater than his fear of fame. This ambition drives him to give up his comfort of being unknown. His ambition of being economically successful in life is greater than his fear of losing his job. That is the mindset of the first dancer. He is willing to let go of his false sense of possession to reach for bigger things in life.

Chapter 4

Attitudinal Leadership: It's Child's Play

When I read the news about the 17-year-old activist from Pakistan, Malala Yousafzai winning the prestigious Nobel Peace Prize, I couldn't but recall the hundreds of nauseatingly clichéd discussions I read and heard as a student on whether leadership is inborn or acquired. What constitutes true nature of leadership?

I wondered why it is that people coming right out of a leadership training would hardly ever have a coherent definition of leadership. None of them would seem to agree on one definition despite having studied the characteristics of leaders in detail. Despite decades of research, we have never quite laid to rest the question of whether it is inborn or acquired.

As a student, I couldn't care less about that question; all I knew was that leadership is an attitude. Whether you are a good leader or not has hardly anything to do with your genetics and everything to do with the attitudes you develop along the way. Bear with me on that thought!

INBORN OR ACQUIRED

When you see so many examples of individuals from prominent families ending up becoming great leaders, you tend to think of that as a general rule. It gets confusing after a while, doesn't it? If one of your parents has been an accomplished leader, you have it in your genes and hence it is natural for you to end up in a position of authority. For one, this is innately oxymoronic–the quality of leadership has nothing to do with being in a position of authority. Secondly, attitudes are cultivated from the seeds of beliefs and beliefs are partly formed through experience.

A child living in a home with parents who are leaders is more likely to develop the core beliefs required to plant the seed of attitudinal leadership, not because this attitude was divinely ordained for her by virtue of her being her parent's child, but merely by having the advantage of experiencing leadership first-hand and acquiring *attitudinal leadership* as a defining element of her personality in the crucial early years.

LEADERSHIP AND AUTHORITY

Attitudinal leadership is what helps us distinguish leadership from authority, what I would refer to as *positional leadership*. A senior manager can be a horrible leader while a school girl can demonstrate exceptional leadership potential in a play group.

Sans the required attitudes, the manager cannot become a true leader who is respected by his team, whereas the attitudinal leadership of the child is highly likely to help her acquire a position of authority in life.

As opposed to the manager who was elevated to a position of authority by another person at a higher position of authority, the child's authority will come from the willingness of her followers to follow her. In other words, attitudinal leadership is what leads to a bottom-up elevation to authority. A leader springs from amongst the masses and elevates to authority on account of her distinguishing attitudes and extricates the followers from the duty to follow the leader. They are not obliged to follow the leader but since the leader's attitudes have reasonable degree of permanence to them, it is likely that they would like to continue following her.

LEARNING ATTITUDINAL LEADERSHIP

Simply put, attitudinal leadership is when you develop the attitude of a leader and end up gaining a leadership position. Positional leadership on the other hand, is when you develop leadership skills *because* you have been assigned to a position of authority. However, for people in positions of authority, it is never too late to learn the attitudes required to become a leader. Since attitudes essentially emanate from a set of core beliefs, it is necessary that a conscientious effort be made to develop the core beliefs that lead to attitudinal leadership.

THE ATTITUDES

It is hard to come up with an exhaustive list of attitudes that constitute attitudinal leadership, but I have a feeling it wouldn't be a long list. Quite often, we tend to get carried away when trying to list the attitudes that *define* a leader. The attitudes that determine whether you have it in you or not are bound to be just a few. And skills like communication or being good at managing time have no place in it. If they did, everyone who possessed these skills would be the greatest leaders in history. All true leaders have the attitudes to acquire those essential skills to become successful at leading, but all who have those essential skills do not become leaders.

Perhaps the most prominent attitude then would be the drive to spearhead change. A true leader is never complacent with the status quo; he is a reformer. He has an insatiable urge to intervene and make a difference, to change something that is not as it is supposed to be. At the same time he is optimistic and persistent.

A leader is passionate about the values he believes in. This passion resonates with his followers and emerges in form of a collective vision for change. His persistence aides to build a momentum which evolves into a voluntary acceptance of the vision by the followers.

Today Malala Yousafzai is known as one of the greatest leaders of our times not because she had it in her genes, but quite simply because her experiences helped her nurture the attitudes that are hallmarks of attitudinal leadership. She believed in her vision, was persistent in her efforts to bring about change and was optimistic about the future.

For the first dancer, leadership is an attitude. It is an insatiable urge to be better; to *do* better. He doesn't wait for his benefactors to put him in charge. His sincere desire to bring about change, coupled with his bias for action, creates a moral authority that obliges people to follow him. He is made a leader by his followers.

As you identify the differentiating attitudes that define attitudinal leadership, I encourage you to think of real life examples of someone you see as leader despite him or her not being in a position of authority.

Chapter 5

Dealing with Rejection

Rejection could be a real bummer for most of us, until we figure out it doesn't have to be. For those of us who've been watching ABC's Shark Tank–or its Canadian twin, Dragon's Den–the statement "for that reason I'm out" is all too familiar. I would guess it is one of the most widely broadcast statements in the history of electronic media in North America, after maybe "I love you" or "you're fired."

As soon as the pitch ends, almost everyone is sure to get a "no" from at least one of the Sharks right off the bat. Some aspirants are out of luck to the extent of being yelled at by a Shark right in middle of the pitch. The fact that the statement is so common points to the uneasy reality of life; it is impossible to completely avoid rejection. I'm afraid that's the way life works.

But then, the good news is, rejection is a sign of progress. It helps you uncover areas of personal growth you never focused on. The best way to make sure you don't ever hear the statement "I'm out" from a Shark again is to never turn the television on and of course to never have the thought of participating in the show. Likewise, the best way to avoid rejection is to not do anything in life. But since you are here reading this book right now, I'm pretty sure doing nothing is not what wakes you up in the morning. Well, you can read on.

While rejections cannot be avoided, there are ways to make the aftermath of rejections less of heartache, and in fact to use it to your advantage.

1. TAKE SOME DOWNTIME

Immediately after a rejection, people generally start mulling over it and continue doing that for days. They tend to feel an urge to pity themselves during that grieving period and end up bruising their self-worth. Realize that during this critical time, you are running the risk of losing your sense of purpose. Your impulse reaction is to give up on the idea for good and never to take a chance again. Beware of this natural reaction to rejection.

The best way to avoid drowning into a slumber of weariness is to take some downtime at the earliest. That doesn't mean you sit idle at home. Quite the opposite; occupy yourself with something fun. Move away from the things that remind you of the negative experience—physically. Take a road trip; get your mind away from what caused your negative reaction. Binge on your favorite dessert. Recoup your verve and re-energize your spirit. You'll need it soon.

2. TALK TO A TRUSTED FRIEND

When you get back to your normal routine and just before you start feeling miserable again, find a trusted friend to talk to. Make sure he or she is someone who has a positive frame of mind. Negativity is the last thing you'd want more of. Let your friend provide constructive feedback; even positive criticism. The reason why hearing objective criticism from a trusted friend works is because you know he or she is not judging you. At the same time your attention is diverted to finding areas of improvement in your strategy rather than to find more people to blame. Internal attribution of failure at this stage is of vital importance. You have to take responsibility of what went wrong before you could figure out how to fix it. More on that in the last point.

3. KNOW THAT REJECTION IS PROGRESSION

It is absolutely fine to think of rejection as a form of failure. But we need to rethink our attitude towards failure. The first thing is to be aware of the fact that failure is inevitable. Not only that, the number of times you fail is directly proportionate to the attempts you make and the chances you take. Most successful people have failed a number of times before they achieved their first big success. Throughout human history, the story of success is punctuated with failures, big and small.

It is important to think of rejection as progression and not regression. It is like walking on a rocky road towards your destination. Every time you hit a rock, you in fact move closer to your destination. There is no guarantee that there wouldn't be any more rocks on the way, but it is important to get up, brush the dust off and continue your forward progression after stumbling on every rock. Just let go and move on. Rejection is progression also because every time you get rejection, you learn what does not work. As Thomas A. Edison said:

> "I have not failed. I've just found 10,000 ways that won't work."

4. DON'T TAKE IT PERSONALLY

The toughest part about dealing with rejection is that you feel your self-esteem crashing down to the floor the moment you hear no. It is a bigger disappointment when you expected to hear yes and worked really hard to deserve it. You cannot help but think of yourself as inadequate and unable to achieve success.

Let's be real. Unless you had a century-old family feud with the person who said no to you, the rejection is not a reflection of a person's absolute judgment about you. They rejected *your proposal or request*, not you. It is important to separate yourself from the subject matter and to not let the rejection hurt your self-perception we discussed in chapter 2. In the business world, you would rarely ever find yourself in a situation where addressing the cause of rejection is beyond your control.

Some people tend to take rejections personally. Again, for them it is a reaffirmation of their low self-worth. Until they build a higher self-esteem and are cognizant of their tendency to take rejection personally, they cannot do much to alleviate it

The reason for rejection is often a misalignment between two people's priorities. When a Shark says "I'm out" to an aspiring entrepreneur, he or she is in fact saying "My objectives don't align with yours." The funny thing is that quite often all Sharks have different reasons for saying no. Each Shark's reason points to why he or she thinks their objectives don't align with the presenter's objectives. It's never personal.

5. THINK OF REJECTIONS AS A WAY TO CHALLENGE YOURSELF

Rejections challenge you, and challenges keep your life interesting. In Cassandra Clare's book, City of Bones, Clary says to Jace, "Have you fallen in love with the wrong person yet?" "Unfortunately, Lady of the Haven," she replies "my one true love remains myself." "At least," Clary says, "you don't have to worry about rejection, Jace Wayland." "Not necessarily. I turn myself down occasionally, just to keep it interesting."

If you have the habit of hearing yes, after a while you tend to lose the spirit of inquiry. Your desire to take up new challenges wanes and with that, your growth halts. Rejection pushes you out of your comfort zone and keeps you from settling for mediocrity. Accepting the challenge that comes with rejection prepares you to knock it out of the park the next time a curveball is thrown at you.

6. USE IT AS AN OPPORTUNITY TO UNLEARN AND RELEARN

After some time has passed and the effect of the bad trip is behind you, you need to get objectively analytical. Think of why you faced rejection. Reflect on what exactly went wrong and how you can fix it. Perhaps all you need is to be more flexible and change your strategy rather than addressing a real deficiency. It could also be just a bad presentation of your ideas, a misunderstanding of common values, or an inaccurate identification of the need. Whatever it is, don't be fixated on repeating what didn't work. Think it through and try to approach the problem differently, all the while focusing on your strengths. In that sense rejection is truly a blessing in disguise as it helps you learn empirically from your experience.

7. CONVINCE YOURSELF THAT IT HAPPENED FOR A GREATER REASON

In the short-run, there's no way to know for sure that the rejection would eventually lead you to a greater good. But convincing yourself that it would, can help you manage the aftermath of rejection and come out on top. This reminds me of an oft-quoted anecdote.

A little girl was holding two apples in her hands. Her mother gently asked her with a smile, "My sweetie, could you give your mum one of your two apples?" The girl looked up at her mother for a few seconds, then she suddenly took a quick bite on one apple, and then quickly on the other. The mother felt the smile on her face freeze. She tried hard not to reveal her disappointment. Then the little girl handed one of her bitten apples to her mother and said, "Mummy, here you are. This is the sweeter one."

In life, what appears to be a rejection or failure is nature's way of saying, "Wait, you deserve better than this." It is wise to think of rejections as opportunities to prepare for bigger successes.

8. LEARN TO REGULATE YOUR EXPECTATIONS

It is great to be optimistic. It helps you bring out the best in you. At the same time however, it makes equally good sense to keep your expectations just low enough to feel adequately challenged and to push yourself to put the best foot forward. Having realistic expectations will force you to prepare your best and increase your chances of success. But even if you eventually face rejection, your *realistically* positive expectations will help you bear the brunt.

Know that what you are attempting to achieve has an element of outstretch to it and hence you need to give it your best shot. Beware however that keeping your expectations too low will drain you of your motivation to try your best. A fine balance between optimism and realism is the key. Be ready to do your best but also to handle the worst.

9. UNDERSTAND YOUR LOCUS OF CONTROL

Your locus of control is the degree to which you believe that you have control over the events that affect you. People with strong internal locus of control believe they can control their life while those with external locus of control believe their life is controlled by the decisions and actions of others and they have limited or no influence on those factors.

In the face of rejection, people with external locus of control lose their self-esteem and tend to undermine their strengths. They doubt their abilities and give up the power to control their own actions as well as the consequences of those actions. It is absolutely vital to be aware of your own locus of control and to understand that an external locus could push you into a downward spiral which would tarnish your self-esteem over the long run. At the same time, it is important to understand that while you can make your best effort and put your strengths to best use, it is not in your control to dictate how people would feel and react.

Your best bet is to focus on what you can do to improve your chances of success and avoid rejection. Control your actions, behaviours and attitudes, and empower yourself to influence the outcome to a reasonable degree.

PART 2
Reinventing Yourself

"Those who cannot change their minds cannot change anything."
—George Bernard Shaw

Chapter 6

Personal Branding: Discover the Brand Called 'You'

The first objective of this chapter is simply to help you answer the fundamental question that comes up long before you even start thinking of how to promote your personal brand—what *is* your brand? Once you have that figured out, promoting your brand becomes a piece of cake. The second intention is to keep it simple and action-oriented. Lastly, it is not intended for personal branding gurus but for the inquisitive minds that want to take charge of their brands for future career success.

THE GENUINE BRAND

While personal branding is now evolving into a structured approach for creating a personal identity and promise of value, the core concept has been there long before Tom Peters coined the phrase "the brand called you" in his famous Fast Company article in 1997. We used to call it "your reputation."

Gone are the days when individuals and companies could get away with cooking up a brand statement as eyewash for getting famous overnight. It is no more only about what you want to portray but what you are that creates and sustains brands, whether personal or corporate. If a chicken wants to brand itself as a cow, it can fix a fake cow tail and learn to moo, but will it start giving milk? Well, if you doubt it, you're not the only one. There goes your brand!

BRAND WORTHY OF REMARK

Tom Peters wrote:

> "The good news—and it is largely good news—is that everyone has a chance to stand out. Everyone has a chance to learn, improve, and build up their skills. Everyone has a chance to be a brand worthy of remark."

Your personal brand is not just a future promise of value, but an expression of your *product features* at present (brand differentiation). Creating a personal brand worthy of remark starts with your core competencies and skill sets that would eventually translate into a credible promise of value (brand credibility).

Your ability and reputation to deliver on your promise of value is what characterizes your brand. In other words, your brand is *what you want people to know about you*. It has to be something useful and relevant to their needs (brand relevance).

People will know what you can do for them in future based on who you are at present. Regardless of how much time and effort you spend on the former, unless the two are aligned, the brand won't fly. Lastly, the way you deliver the value has to be sustainable (brand sustainability).

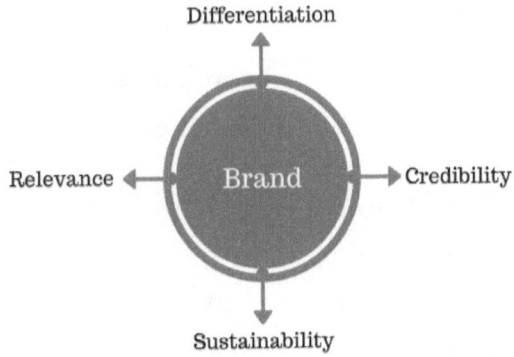

ORGANIZATIONAL CAPABILITY

Let's work on differentiation and credibility first. Start by asking yourself the following questions:

- What do I know about myself?
- What do people know about me?

Let's call the answers to the above questions, your *organizational capability* just so that it's in line with what you studied in business school.

Now we'll do a little exercise to arrive at your genuine brand which you would be able to use as your identity consistently across all channels, online and offline.

STEP 1: WHAT YOU KNOW ABOUT YOURSELF

Take a piece of paper and list everything that describes you from interests and hobbies to personality traits and achievements. It could be adjectives, nouns, phrases; it doesn't matter as long as you are true to yourself. Let's call them attributes for the sake of consistency. Here's a sample:

- Photography
- Public Speaking
- Communicative
- Storytelling
- Honour student
- Rock climbing
- Hanging out with friends
- Make people happy
- Big picture person
- Entrepreneurial

Once you have this done, move on to the next question.

STEP 2: WHAT PEOPLE KNOW ABOUT YOU

If you think you'd be able to create a personal brand only on the basis of what you know about yourself, you are mistaken. What your friends come up with might surprise you to say the least. Besides, no matter what you think of yourself, your brand is what others think of you. That is your real reputation. It is imperative that you know it to be able to build on it or do something to change it. Finding an answer to this question is like having a focus group with clients to determine your company's brand personality–the company being Me Inc.

Selecting your focus group is critical. You do not want to reach out to people who hold a grudge against you for being the top student throughout college or to the ones who are too nice to be honest. I suggest you pick five people who have known you for at least a few years and approach them separately with your question. Give them some time to think it through and ask them to email you the list of five to seven attributes they think describe you the best. I have illustrated three lists below.

Friend 1

- Fun loving
- Eye for beauty
- Good time manager
- Emotional
- Easily bored
- Social

Friend 2

- Independent at work
- Meeting new people
- Helpful
- Committed to goals
- Honest
- Appreciate art
- Driven by success

Friend 3

- Future oriented
- Outdoor person
- Creative
- Lack of focus
- Love adventure
- Altruistic
- Organized

STEP 3: FIND COMMON ELEMENTS

Now that you have your own list of personal attributes and a list of attributes that your friends think you possess, it is time to put them all together.

Take the five lists (three in my illustration) from step 2. Put together the attributes that appear more than once (regardless of your friends' choice of words). This would give you the following new list:

- Fun loving, outdoor person, love adventure
- Eye for beauty, appreciate art, creative
- Good time manager, committed to goals, driven by success, organized
- Easily bored, lack of focus
- Social, meeting new people
- Helpful, altruistic

It appears that you already have a brand without even knowing about it. The list summarizes what your reputation is. Now it is time to take charge of your reputation and build it into a consistent, sustainable personal brand.

STEP 4: ADD YOUR PERSONAL LENS

Once you have the list of common attributes that your friends came up with, add the relevant attributes from it to your own list of personal attributes. But this time do something more. For every attribute in your own list that also appears in the lists from step 3, mark it with letter 'A'.

Leave the attributes unmarked from your own list that do not feature in your friends' list of common attributes (the last four items in the example below).

- Photography, eye for beauty, appreciate art, creative – 'A'
- Honour student, driven by success, good time manager, organized – 'A'
- Rock climbing, fun loving, outdoor person, love adventure – 'A'
- Hanging out with friends, social, meetings new people – 'A'
- Make people happy, helpful, altruistic – 'A'
- Big picture person, easily bored, lack of focus – 'A'
- Entrepreneurship
- Public speaking
- Communicative
- Storytelling

STEP 5: DISCOVER YOUR BRAND

For all the unmarked attributes at the bottom of the above list, look for the attributes from the original three lists your friends sent that closely match the former. Add them to your list from step 4 and mark them with letter 'B'.

- Photography, eye for beauty, appreciate art, creative – 'A'
- Honour student, driven by success, good time manager, organized – 'A'
- Rock climbing, fun loving, outdoor person, love adventure – 'A'

- Hanging out with friends, social, meetings new people – 'A'
- Make people happy, helpful, altruistic – 'A'
- Big picture person, easily bored, lack of focus – 'A'
- Entrepreneurship, independent at work, future oriented – 'B'
- Public speaking
- Communicative
- Storytelling, emotional – 'B'

You're almost there. The attributes you marked with the letter 'A' are your primary attributes and the ones you marked with the letter 'B' are your secondary attributes. Omit the unmarked attributes. Now sort them as such and add a statement in front of each to describe what you think it really means.

- Photography, eye for beauty, appreciate art, creative – *I have good visualization skills*
- Honour student, driven by success, good time manager, organized – *I am disciplined and competitive*
- Rock climbing, fun loving, outdoor person, love adventure – *I am a risk taker*
- Hanging out with friends, social, meetings new people – *I love interacting with people*

- Make people happy, helpful, altruistic – *I can help and motivate people*
- Big picture person, easily bored, lack of focus – *I am a big picture person*
- Entrepreneurship, independent at work, future oriented – *I like to be my own boss*
- Storytelling, emotional – *I am empathetic*

Guess what, you have just found your personal attributes that characterize your brand. That's great! But remember, we were only talking of the organizational capability aspect and not the whole brand.

ADD BRAND POSITIONING & BUSINESS STRATEGY TO THE EQUATION

Let's go back to our discussion on differentiation, credibility, relevance and sustainability. You have already solved for differentiation and credibility by answering the two questions: what you know about yourself and what people know about you (organizational capability). The next step is to find out your brand relevance and make it sustainable.

The attributes (reflecting organizational capability) that you just came up with, point to your ability to deliver value. These may or may not be the brand attributes that would create the promise of value you want to communicate to your client or employer. Your organizational capability has to be aligned with your desired brand positioning and business strategy to arrive at a concrete personal brand that entails who you are, what value you offer and how you offer it.

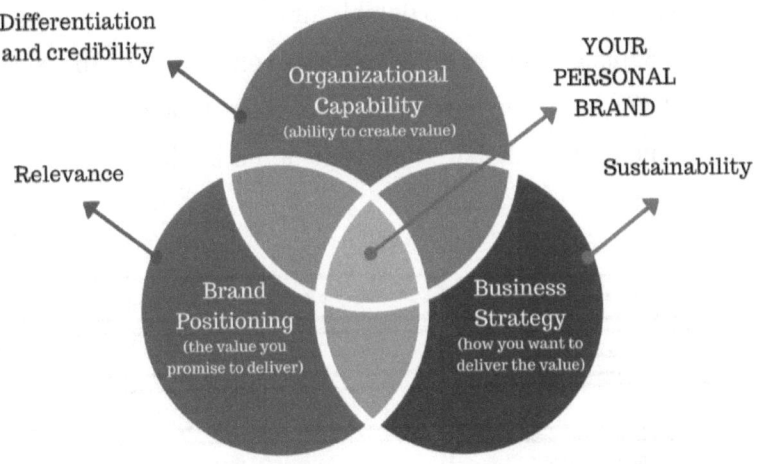

BRAND POSITIONING – WHERE YOUR PROMISE OF VALUE LIES

Your brand positioning is what gives relevance to your brand and sets you apart from your competition. For the discussion on differentiation and credibility you didn't need to look into the specifics of your industry, your clients, your employer or your business title. You were only focused on your personal attributes and abilities regardless of their relevance to your professional or business domain. Brand positioning is what translates your brand attributes into relevant promise of value for your audience.

Let's work off the brand attributes we came up with. For each of the brand attributes, come up with one or more 'I can' statements. That will translate your *ability to deliver value* into *actual value* that is relevant for your client or employer (your audience). For that you have to understand the audience and your business domain first.

Suppose you are an advertising consultant for the retail industry. As such, you have to position your brand as relevant to that domain but only based on your brand attributes. Let's try doing that.

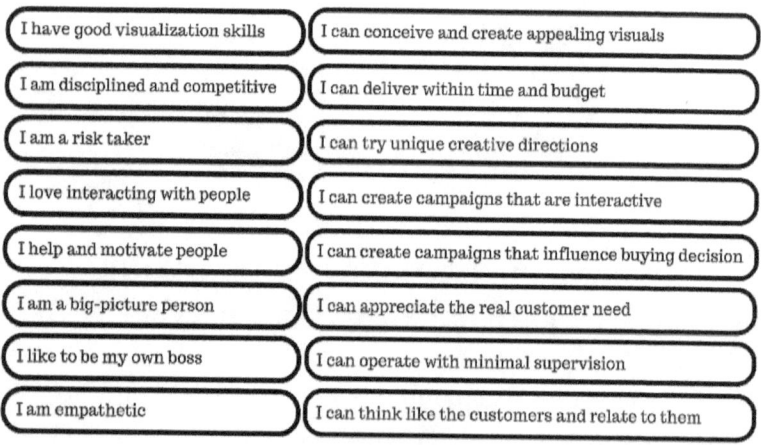

The above list of values you promise to deliver is now relevant to your audience. And since you started off with trying to differentiate yourself based on credible brand attributes that collectively set you apart from your competition, what you have at this stage is relevant, differentiated and credible. You can now chart these on a typical brand positioning grid and see where you are vis-à-vis your competition.

BUSINESS STRATEGY – HOW YOU WANT TO DELIVER YOUR VALUE

Your personal brand is incomplete without the third critical element: your business strategy. This can be based on the tools, technologies, processes and talents you will use to deliver your brand value. It will give you the anchor to make your brand sustainable over time.

For each of your personal 'I can' statements from the brand positioning exercise, add a 'how' phrase. Let's try doing that for some of the statements:

- I can deliver within time and budget - because of my impeccable track record and expertise in using advanced project management tools
- I can try unique creative directions - having worked with the best creative talent in the advertising industry
- I can create campaigns that are interactive - using the latest multimedia and web-based technologies
- I can create campaigns that influence the buying decision - due to deep customer insights and experience with innovative research methodologies

Voilà! You just got yourself a personal brand that you can now tailor into an expression of your liking, visual, verbal or any other way you like. Go create your own blog, have a personal logo or a tagline; blow yourself away with all the amazing articles on how to give expression to your personal brand and put it out there for the world to see. It is your true identify—one you should be proud of.

It will differentiate you from others and give your career or business the boost it deserves. Just remember that branding—whether personal or corporate—is not a gimmick. It is an expression of who you are at present and what you can do in the future. My advice: keep it at that.

Chapter 7

Building an Attitude of Credibility

Whatever your personal definition of success is, you have to make sure that people are willing to trust you if you want to achieve success in life. This is one of the most basic prerequisites of success regardless of the field of work you are in or your position in an organization.

It is important because every day we find ourselves in situations where we need to persuade people to do something. Needless to say, a person would not feel comfortable doing what you want her to do, unless she trusts you enough. We generally believe that in order to nurture trust in relationships, we need to invest considerable time and effort to build a certain rapport with people so that we are in a position to influence their behaviour.

While this might sound like a lot of hard work for most people, some people are simply hardwired to build strong credibility with anyone they meet. They are able to do that because they do not only spend time building trust in each relationship, but also developing the 'attitude of credibility' as part of their character. The truth is, anyone who is willing to consistently invest time in building the core attitudes of credibility can get 'hardwired' to be an influencer.

1. BE TRUE TO WORD

Nothing can tarnish your credibility more than your failure to keep your promise. If you promised to send that email to the client by 4:00 pm, make sure you do it by that time. People are willing to overlook a lapse as an exception and not as the norm. Also, if you are truly determined to consistently follow through on your commitments, make sure you do not over-promise. It makes it easier to stand by your promises. More on that in point number 7.

2. GET SOMEONE ELSE TO BLOW YOUR HORN

Few of us would voluntarily sit around and listen to some braggart go on and on about how wonderful he/she is. Still, every so often, we may be tempted to flatter ourselves by telling the world what great things we have accomplished. Before you start conjuring up diabolical imagery associated with bragging, let me wholeheartedly admit that; kept within limits, some "horn blowing" can produce positive effects ranging from admiration to opportunities for success.

However, if you *"get someone else to blow your horn, the sound will carry twice as far."* Consider the difference between "I'm the most dependable member of the team" and "Ben is the most dependable member of *my* team." Both statements seem to carry the same meaning but they are completely different in terms of their degree of effectiveness in building Ben's credibility.

It is like *influence marketing* where you get a celebrity to praise your product or service. When people see the product being used and endorsed by someone else (in this case a person who people trust and admire), the message suddenly becomes more credible.

3. LEARN TO SAY 'I DON'T KNOW'

In the age of the Internet, we feel like we are expected to know the answer to every question right off the bat. As a result of feeling compelled to come across as knowledgeable, we have become accustomed to answer questions based on a few facts and a lot of guesswork. Ironically, research has become so easy that many of us have stopped making a real effort to find answers to questions. Also, once we have blurted out a harebrained answer to a question, we lose the motivation to find the real answer. But let's be clear; simply saying that you don't know the answer but you're willing to find out actually makes you look smart and scrupulous. Provided you do get back with an answer later, saying you don't know helps you establish yourself as a credible source of knowledge.

4. GIVE, NOT TAKE

A social interaction is typically a transaction in which two people exchange something of value. In many cases, the value you derive from an interaction is an agreement by the other person to do what you would like him or her to do. However, to cut the first turf in a conversation and create trust, you should take the lead and make it adequately clear that you are genuinely interested in providing something of value to the person across the table. If right at the beginning of the conversation, your body language, your intonations, your choice of words are all aligned to give that impression, you have done half the job at building lasting credibility.

5. LISTEN WELL

Active listening does an incredible job at creating trust. When people are speaking, give them your full attention, and ask questions to clarify anything that you don't understand. It is more important to be interested than interesting. People with poor listening skills and a habit to interject often, find it hard to influence people to do things out of their free will.

6. USE SIMPLE LANGUAGE

Being eloquent or knowledgeable doesn't mean overusing jargon. In fact, the more you know about a subject and the more passionately you feel like talking to people about it, the more inclined you are to use words that communicate the core idea in the most articulate form. It goes to show that you are making an authentic effort to transfer the idea into the listener's mind as accurately as possible. This helps build credibility for the content of your message as well as for your intent to communicate.

7. QUALITY OVER QUANTITY

It is easy to work too much (or too little); striking a balance between quantity and quality is what is hard to do. People who have an attitude of credibility are focused on few things in life—things they really want to excel at. Rather than taking up a number of activities at once, try to be the best at one thing. Learn to turn down offers that distract you from excelling at that one thing. This will help you make sure you do not over promise in terms of the quantity of work you can do (and hence make it easier to keep your promises). At the few things you are focused on, even do so much as going beyond the call of duty in order to excel and build an impression of commitment. Over time, this would establish your credibility as an expert in the area.

8. BE ACCOUNTABLE FOR YOUR FAILURES

People you want to trust are not the ones who blame everyone for the results of their actions. Quite the contrary, they take full ownership of the consequences of their decisions, especially if they result in failure. They are equally openhearted in giving credit for their successes to those who contributed, however little, in helping them achieve their successes. Putting blame on others gives people the impression that you would be on the lookout for scapegoats should your next venture fail. That would be enough to tarnish your credibility.

9. DRESS TO BUILD CREDIBILITY

You have to make sure that you look the kind of person that a customer would like to give money to. A huge part of the first impression you make is based on how your dress. Now that's not too hard to achieve. Every detail matters when it comes to *looking* credible. Dressing that evokes an impression of strength, trust and confidence tell people that you are willing to play the part and do whatever it takes to be successful (refer to 'perception of success' in chapter 11). You come across as serious, detailed-oriented and dependable. Chapter 10 takes a look at the power of the visual from another perspective.

10. FOCUS ON THE COMMON

The quintessential advice for sales conversations is to build a rapport with the potential client by talking about things that the two of you share in common. It could be anything from a hobby to the same alma mater. Strangely, this helps people suspend the disbelief and make them *want to believe you*. Human mind works in intriguing ways. By only bringing up a topic that creates a common bond with your audience, you suddenly become more trustworthy than you were in absence of that common bond. I would be more inclined to listen to someone from my hometown than to a person from a strange land.

***

The way the first dancer is able to attract unlimited opportunities for success is by making people open up to him more than they would to others. That is possible only because the first dancer comes across as someone they can trust. He ingrains the ten attributes of the attitude of credibility as an inalienable part of his character and through their consistent application, he is able to build a reputation of being trustworthy.

Chapter 8

You Are Who You Know: My Experience with Networking

When fisherman Jack finally landed a boot, he knew it was the last straw. His spectacular skills, with the perfect fishing gear, which he'd gone to great lengths to polish each day for the past 20 years, were no longer working. Jack was exasperated. He suffered from cold feet, itchy fingers and a hunger for success which drove him to pursue each boot with a vengeance. Jack was out of his element, and as much as he had always admired boots, he realized something that day, which changed his life forever.

Now consider this—new in the country, six months flushed down in hope of finding suitable work and hard earned savings disappearing like quicksilver in the cracks. Add this to throw in a bit of twist—no contacts. Like Jack, I felt like I had hit rock bottom.

So between my episodes of frantic quibbling and blaming anybody I could get hold of, I did the obvious thing anyone would do–I surfed the net. I spent the greater part of each day searching for vacancies in banking, where I knew everything inside out. I just needed to let people see that, and everything would turn out just fine.

Although I knew deep inside that applying for positions online was an unlikely bet anywhere, let alone in the very competitive Toronto job market, I continued mulishly for lack of knowledge of anything better to do. What sparked my egotistic determination was the plethora of advice on relocating to another city or going back to school, or even worse; changing occupation. All advices were targeted to the *what* my goal should be and not to the *how* to achieve the goal I had.

A few thousand dollars later, someone I ran into at an event told me how smart networking helped one of his friends land a great job. That was of course not the first time my attention had been drawn to this potent alchemy but as all new immigrants like to think, it was something of interest to those few devious job hunters who loved long hauls rather than being forthright in approaching prospective employers directly, which I always thought was the shortest route to success.

Besides, what could be better than sitting in the cushy warmth of my home in the December of Toronto; the coldest in six years; and posting my off-the-shelf resume to one employer after the other. For me, churning out many applications in little time was the recipe for success. Targeted marketing was in my view something reserved for the textbooks and impracticable seminar presentations. But quite frankly, I was just hoping to get lucky and hit the jackpot while I stayed in my comfort zone. Quantity over quality was my formula for success.

In hindsight, I'm so glad I visited the event that day. Not only for the motivation which continues to drive me, not for the brief respite from my efforts, but quite simply, for forcing me to come face to face with the bitter truth about my own ways. It was an eye-opener more than anything else–a nudge that compelled me to think. I finally realized that while I liked thinking of myself as persevering, I had been too afraid to fail, and hence to try. Perseverance for me was no longer about being stupid or stubborn. Now it was all about being flexible and adaptable while sticking to my goal. It was the 'how' that changed, not the 'what.'

The little things I have learned about smart networking can easily be summed up in this chapter but what cannot be expressed in words is the power of positive attitude. Hence, as you read through these no-rocket-science tips from my personal experience viewpoint, keep the underlying code of positive attitude as your guiding principle.

HAVE A PLAN

Before I jumped right into it, I jotted down my 'things to do.' My smart networking plan was simply the list of social activities I wanted to engage in so as to create and cultivate my own network, along with an estimate of time and money each activity would require. The idea was to make sure I didn't miss out on the things that might turn out to be most effective later on.

The list included activities like joining a community volunteer program, my neighborhood soccer team, a study group in my local library, connecting with people through social media and regularly visiting my place of worship. I had a balanced plan in that it didn't skew too much towards one or two activities while ignoring others. Once I had listed down my activities, I put them on my calendar with specific dates and hours of day so that it would become my routine. But then, I did not take my timetable to heart. After all, it was about being flexible, right?

JOIN NETWORKING GROUPS

My plan was to try and get as many memberships as I could afford. I couldn't afford any so I looked around for the free ones or tagged along with others to networking events. For me, it answered an important how question—how to start my smart networking. I didn't have to buy expensive memberships to professional associations; I only went online and joined groups and forums which were interactive and had physical presence too.

I looked for groups that would meet up every so often to exchange ideas and help members connect at a personal level to build rapport. In my search of the common element that creates the bond between two persons, being member of the same group was perhaps the easiest one to have—the low hanging fruit in the tree of smart networking if you will. However, I had a genuine interest in what the groups stood for and I was selective in deciding which ones to join.

ATTEND NETWORKING EVENTS

What worked for me was meeting the same people twice at important events. Sometimes, it cemented my fragile connections into strong bonds that would last a lifetime. For me, it was crucial to be seen and be heard, to speak up and make an impression—a positive one. I knew that face-to-face interactions would either make it or break it for me, but I was not afraid of failing anymore.

For me, the 30 minutes or so of informal networking time before and after the formal event were crucial. I tried and made the most of my time. Every minute counted. As I engaged in small talk with new people, I tried to get a sense of their inclinations. I evaluated them as much as they evaluated me. If I got caught in a meaningless conversation with a less-than-ideal networker, I didn't stick it out. I concluded my conversation politely and moved on to the next person.

I made it a point to exchange business cards at the end of my conversation with everyone and anyone I met. Regardless of how futile the interaction seemed to me at first, I didn't know what might work. I didn't know who my second- or third-degree connection would be (people that my first-degree connection will introduce me to). That's the funny thing about networking.

It is not only the one-one-one connection that is important but also how your network expands through that first connection. And yes, paying a few bucks to register for events is money well spent.

PRACTICE PUBLIC SPEAKING

I realized that being good at public speaking would draw my contacts to me rather than I needing to go out to them. But I had always thought of public speaking as a challenge and not as an opportunity. This is where my guiding principle helped me out most. I knew it was unlikely that I would be asked to deliver a speech to an audience impromptu, so I didn't expect that, but I was always on the lookout for every opportunity to speak without looking childishly eager to do so. At events, I elegantly volunteered to express my opinions when asked.

This was of course only possible once I was prepared enough to make the right impression. I didn't take the risk when I had no clue what I was going to say on the subject. But then, I had to take the risk in order to practice. So when confronted with the question, what's the best way to practice public speaking, joining forums like Toastmasters was my answer. That was the place where everyone was taking the risk and there was no shame if I did too. The more I practiced, the higher was my risk threshold and confidence level, and hence more the practice I got. It was like a spiral.

Once I had enough confidence to step up to the podium and say a few words at an event, I did it. I did not wait forever to become a master at public speaking. That would have taken me an age. All I needed was only that little amount of confidence to walk up to the podium. My preparation would take it from there.

WARM IT UP WITH COLD EMAILS

Before I got my first success at finding a job in Canada, I thought the power of LinkedIn was overrated. It is! LinkedIn might not land you a job per se, but it sure can help you get an abundant supply of information interviews with people who can connect you with prospective employers within their network or outside.

I considered myself lucky to receive a 25% response to my LinkedIn emails, while some 10% called me for a chat over coffee. That was my cue to shine. But before I reached to that point, I organized my effort and had a list of contacts available with valid email addresses. I got a basic paid LinkedIn account to be able to send emails to people outside of my immediate network. I drafted a polite yet assertive email focusing on what was common between me and my prospective contact and had the draft reviewed by friends to get a second opinion.

To personalize my standard email draft, I went through the intended recipient's LinkedIn profile to find out what interested him or her, professionally and personally. If I couldn't find anything better, I would join a group on LinkedIn that my potential contact was already a member of, and start my email with that. Sometimes it worked, sometimes it didn't.

But that was my best bet. While writing to people on LinkedIn, I would always write to offer help rather than to narrate my sob story and I would always remember to close with a strong call to action.

And remember there is nothing wrong with reaching out to complete strangers if you follow the rules of networking and the norms of civilized discourse.

BE RESPONSIVE, BE AVAILABLE

Whether it was answering my emails, or receiving voicemails, travelling to meet someone for an information interview or sorting my snail mail, I was well organized. It helped me save my time and that of others. To me, it was not only courteous to respond to every correspondence within reasonable time, it was the moral right of the person I was communicating with. I knew that perhaps this was the only place where my first impression could get overridden by the second.

By the same token, I made sure I arrived at meetings in time. I mostly took public transit, so I purchased a monthly pass rather than carrying jiggling pockets to the station only to find out I was short of change. And arriving 10 minutes early at the venue never hurt. If unavailable to take calls, a nice voicemail greeting recorded on my phone would greet the caller. Also, I made it a point to check my voice messages and get back to the callers within 24 hours, unless it was more urgent than that.

SEE HOW YOU LOOK ONLINE

A senior mentor once told me, "everyone Googles everyone." Weeks later, I was enthralled by how true he was about the strange phenomenon we are now growing accustomed to. It was so funny when I knew that somebody I was meeting apparently for the first time had already been to my Facebook profile. What was funnier was that she was playing it down by pretending that I was someone brand new to her. It was funny because it showed.

But that's not the point. The important thing is that I was aware of this phenomenon and was always careful when creating or updating my online presence. Good or bad, I knew my online presence was as much a part of my existence as my physical being; perhaps not so in reality. But then who cares about reality; it is the perception that counts.

HAVE A NETWORKING TOOLKIT

To make sure the big thing works out for me, I made sure I had the little ones in control. Here's a list of the basic toolkit I used:

Business card

I didn't have to be working at a company to have my business cards. I printed customized cards that mentioned my core professional expertise and had my phone number and email address printed clearly at the bottom. I got help of free online tools for the first batch. My rule was: the simpler the better.

LinkedIn profile

I subscribed to an entry-level paid account at LinkedIn to become more visible to prospective employers. I could see who viewed my profile and send emails to people outside of my immediate network.

Personal website

A couple of years ago, I created a personal website to establish my brand, something I should have done long ago. Through my website, my personal brand helps me stand out from everyone else. It is an expression of what is unique about me. In order to determine my brand positioning for the website, I asked each of my five closest friends to list five qualities they see in me as the most prominent. The one thing that got repeated most was what they commonly identified me as. It became my brand identity. Unless it is something negative, build your personal brand around it and put it out there for the world to see. Chapter 6 outlines a step by step process to create your personal brand.

Thank you cards

I can't overestimate the power of the thank you card. It worked wonders. How I made others feel was how they were likely to want to make me feel. I made them feel valued, and I was sincere in doing that.

If you had a really important meeting with a person and it had strategic importance for you, a personalized thank you card trumps the customary thank you email. It helps you stand out and be remembered.

Voicemail greeting

I wanted to sound professional and courteous but not sheepishly polite. I had a brief recording to greet the caller and I remembered to say thanks and that I would get back to him or her soon. And I did get back soon.

Wardrobe and grooming

I invested some money on my wardrobe. I had a few good business suits in there. They didn't have to be expensive, but had to look good on me and make me feel comfortable and confident. I didn't want to let my tendency for sartorial experimentation get the better of me, so I didn't take the risk of dressing unconventionally or too casually. I didn't want to stand out for the wrong reason. Lastly, I paid attention to my personal grooming. Details mattered.

REMEMBER TO...

Update your list of contacts

After each meeting, I would get as much information down on a piece of paper as I could–name, organization, title, interests and hobbies, where I met them and so forth. Yes even the gender was important. I didn't want to end up reminiscing Daryl as the helpful guy I met at Tim Horton's. I also kept my list handy in case I got a call from Daryl and couldn't recall how I know him, sorry her.

Make critical contacts last a lifetime

I focused on quality, not quantity. I connected with only as many people as I could stay in touch with on a positive note. I tried not to forget the people who helped me and the ones who didn't. I was thankful to all and made sure I expressed my gratitude. I met my contacts once in a while even after I was successful in my immediate goal of finding a job. You never know where it might take you.

Be true to yourself

Saying that perception is bigger than reality did not absolve me of my responsibility to be honest. I was emphatic about my strengths and did not let my weaknesses show, but I never lied. That was the whole idea of building perception that worked for me. While I was busy working on my weaknesses, I was working on being self-aware of my strengths as well. In my interactions with people, I preferred being myself rather than being what I was not. Having said that, I was the best 'me' I possibly could.

Offer help

I was reciprocal in my attitude towards others. No matter what situation I was in, I offered help to people in whatever way I could. In many cases I ended up being the one who got helped.

In my emails, I would not write I needed work. If I had to say it, I said how I could help. It was in the way I said it.

One afternoon on my way back from an information interview, I met a passerby at the bus stop asking for direction. He was visibly new to Canada and needed help. Despite being the last person who could help another newcomer, I offered help and exchanged contact information after our brief introduction. Later that day, I got a call from him saying that he was off to an interview when we met, and since the position in question was not all that relevant to his past experience, he recommended my name for the position. And guess what, I got the call in a couple of days.

For me, social interaction was a transaction, an exchange of value. My willingness to help was like a promissory note I signed to show my commitment to transmit something of value back to the person in future when receiving something of value in the present. And in my whole equation of give and take, give always preceded take.

Be the shameless networker

This required some self-motivation initially. I would often say to myself, "If you are too shy to go out and meet people, don't. But know that there is no shame in initiating a social transaction." I was after all promising to return the value I received at a future date. Once that realization seeped in, I didn't hesitate to approach the speakers for a warm handshake and an expression of thanks after a wonderful conference I attended.

Customize your smart networking plan

I welcomed all the advice I received, but I did only what suited my circumstances best. When preparing my networking plan, I omitted the activities that had very little likelihood of being useful for me. Instead, I filled the list up with more effective means of connecting with people. For me, job fairs didn't work all so well, so I attended them only when I had no better activity on my list and didn't want to keep shooting in the dark by applying online and being at the mercy of not-so-intelligent job search portals.

Step out of the comfort zone

I learned that the moment one starts feeling too comfortable, he or she stops growing as a person. I had to be tough if I wanted to get going. It was never too late to put the lid on my laptop and set up my first real meeting. I was pleasantly surprised to see how eager people were to help, or rather, to transact with me.

Stepping out of my comfort zone helped me in ways I least expected to work. Upon someone's insistence, I joined a full-time course at an employment agency. Initially skeptical of how being stuck in a classroom for seven hours a day could help, I soon realized how much I needed to learn to become job-ready in a new country. After a month of training at the agency, when I finally found myself face-to-face with a prospective employer at a mentoring event, it all came together for me. I was for once at the right place at the right time, and I made the best use of my five minutes. That prospective employer is now my present employer.

Stand out from the crowd
I had kept the cliché for the end. Whatever I did, I didn't limit myself to what everyone else was doing. After all, the whole idea of networking was to be noticed as someone better than my competitors.

All tips aside, what worked for me personally was the high expectation I had of myself. Only because I believed I could achieve the end in mind, I applied the right means to achieve it. Self-fulfilling prophesies, it turns out, are just as prevalent when leading yourself as they are when leading others.

Chapter 9

Know When to Keep Your Mouth Shut

An important element in reinventing yourself to be the first dancer is knowing when not to speak. Many years ago during my short stint at a PR firm, we flew to a client to make a presentation. Minutes after we arrived, a senior executive walked up to us and told us that our key contact at the company passed away last night. To that, my boss impulsively snapped, "Well, didn't you do your succession planning? We flew up here and expect to present to someone." Trying not to look at the utterly stupefied face of the poor guy, I could only hear ear-numbing silence following that short retort from my boss. I vaguely remember a bird or two chirping at a distance too.

Well, I do admire all facets of verbal communication skills and am highly respectful of everyone who takes eloquence and articulation to the next level. But more often than not, it is the failure to appreciate *when to keep quiet* that lands most people in trouble. For discerning employers, a finely honed sense of when not to talk is a highly sought-after communication skill—one that is hard to come by. As someone so aptly put it:

> *"The ability to speak several languages is an asset, but the ability to keep your mouth shut in any language is priceless."*

From my humbling experience of the past many years, here's a list of seven reasons why—and when—to keep your mouth shut:

1. LISTEN, OBSERVE AND LEARN

The greatest business lessons are learnt when you are not talking, but listening. It is a proven fact that if you are talking or thinking of what to say when the other person finishes the sentence, you are not listening to what is being said.

This is because listening is not hearing. It is a cognitive exercise that requires concentration to process the knowledge being imparted. How well you can interpret that knowledge depends largely on your level of concentration and impartial attention. You cannot fake it. Your attention has to come from a genuine desire to understand the message and show that you are sincerely interested in comprehending the real meaning of what's being said. I like how Cheryl Conner put it:

> *"There is a power in listening to others without interruption in order to fully understand what they are saying—to fully understand what they are not saying—and to ensure that they know they are heard."*

2. DO NOT SPEAK ONLY TO CRITICIZE

If you feel the urge to speak up only to sneer at someone's failure or shortcoming with no constructive intent to it, it is better to keep quiet. This is not to say that you should never criticize someone within the accepted norms of social discourse. It only means that in business meetings, criticizing an individual with intent to belittle him or her is not a good idea simply because the negative intent tends to become evident the more you speak. This applies to shifting the blame to an adversary or to someone you have to settle a score with.

> *"Abilities wither under fault-finding, blossom under encouragement."* —Donald A. Laird

If you are a born mentor and coach who can't refrain from pointing out areas of improvement, make sure you do that in one-on-one meetings only after building a strong rapport with the individual. If you are truly concerned about the person's contribution to the organization, the focus should be on offering solutions rather than on rubbing it in his face.

3. DO NOT SPEAK WHEN ANGRY

Like listening, speaking is a cognitive process. The MIT Encyclopedia of the Cognitive Sciences says, "It seems plausible to maintain that universal tendencies in language are grounded in the way we are; this must be so for speaking is a cognitive capacity, that capacity in virtue of which we say that we *know* our native language."

Performance of a cognitive skill hinges on the capacity of the brain to function normally. The data coming into our brain from the world around us passes through the amygdala where the decision is made whether to send the data to the limbic area or frontal lobe of the cerebral cortex. The latter assesses consequences of our actions and is likely what's keeping you from hurling a vase across the room. If the incoming data triggers enough of an emotional charge, amygdala sends the data to the limbic system causing the person to react without much regard for the consequences.

> *"Speak when you are angry–and you'll make the best speech you'll ever regret."*
> —Lawrence J. Peter

Simply put, we are not in our right mind when we are angry. Regardless of whether your anger is justified or not, it is highly advisable to wait for the storm to pass before you see the bright sun of your cognition shining in your head again. Speaking your mind before the frontal lobe takes over is akin to driving when drunk. All you'll end up with is truckload of regret and a few broken hearts. Not to mention, I have seen people losing their jobs only because they spoke when they should have kept quiet.

4. DO NOT SPEAK TO SPREAD RUMORS

Rumors are short-lived. They eventually get discovered as lies and when that happens, all those who took part in spreading the false news move a step closer to losing their credibility. Blabbermouths are always looked down upon in a professional work environment or in a civilized social setting even when they really want to believe what they are saying is true. Doubting everything is a sign of wisdom; speaking your doubts is mere stupidity.

By the same token, saying something while at the same time expressing your doubt about it harms your professional integrity. It is better not to speak if you are unsure whether what you are going to say is the truth and you did not have a chance to confirm the piece of information. Rather than saying "I *think* the survey results were largely positive and we can start developing the marketing campaign" you can simply take away the question and confirm the survey results in the next meeting.

5. DO NOT SPEAK TO STATE THE OBVIOUS

In business meetings or in social discourse, stating the obvious is a suicidal faux-pas that went out of style centuries ago. It only serves to demonstrate that you are an uber-naive person going through an intellectual challenge keeping pace with the discussion.

Same goes for reading your PowerPoint slides verbatim. Irrespective of how verbose the slides are, present the context of the phrase and what meaning you want to convey rather than reading out the exact phrase. If you do not have anything to say about the why and how of the text written on the slides, what is the point of making the presentation in the first place? Consider sending the file as an attachment to save time and effort.

There is an exception to this. If you are stating the obvious only to build the premise for the point you are about to make, go for it by all means. However, make sure your premise is quickly followed by the argument you want to make.

6. CONSERVE ENERGY FOR ACTION

Speaking is an energy-consuming exercise, but when it comes to expressing your intentions too early, speaking becomes an energy-depleting exercise. Once you have apprised people of your intentions, it gives you a "premature sense of completeness."

You have identity triggers in your brain that contribute to your self-image every time an event occurs. Since both actions and speech activate your identity triggers to shape your self-image one bit at a time, talking satisfies the brain enough to neglect the pursuit of action triggers. It is a common observation that announcing your intentions ahead of time satisfies your need to create a particular self-image just enough to lessen the motivation needed to achieve it.

NYU psychology professor Peter Gollwitzer has been studying this since his book "Symbolic Self-Completion" published in 1982. Published results reveal that people who keep their intentions private are more likely to achieve them than those who made them public and were acknowledged by others. Josemaría Escrivá wrote in his 1934 book, The Way:

> *"The fruitfulness of silence! All the energy I see you waste with those repeated indiscretions is energy taken from the effectiveness of your work.*
> *Be discreet."*

7. BUILD POWER THROUGH SILENCE

People with high self-esteem measure up the meaningfulness of a conversation against their self-value before jumping in. I have never seen an accomplished senior executive passing on a lame joke he heard in the elevator. In business meetings, every time you choose not to contribute to a meaningless discourse, it subliminally creates a perception in the minds of others that your contribution to a discussion is truly valuable and they will be eager to hear what you have to say the next time you speak.

Practicing it consistently strengthens this perception and builds your intellectual self-worth. Avoiding meaningless talk in business meetings creates respect from colleagues. Of course overdoing it would make you look rude and aloof. So it is important to have a reasonable threshold of what constitutes meaningfulness.

The first dancer is someone people genuinely want to listen to. Their desire is not out of a compulsion to pay attention to him but as a means to reciprocate the respect he accords to them through his communication skills. He truly values what others have to say and he makes sure it shows by the way he listens to them. He influences people not only by is words but by his silence as well.

Chapter 10

Power of the Visual: We Hear With Our Eyes

Our Physics teacher was more of an older friend for us than a teacher. He took all the boredom away from an arduous science subject by making it incredibly appealing to our curious minds.

He knew extremely well how to communicate complex scientific concepts to us through riveting demonstrations and fascinating experiments (that didn't always work, mind you). The classroom was our playground when it was time to 'study' Physics. The captivating visual appeal of what I was told was Physics, worked wonders to teach me seemingly intricate ideas about the macrocosm and microcosm that have stuck with me to this day. And this is how I learned that light travels faster than sound. Why I still ended up becoming a banker and not a physicist, is a story for another book.

Light is human beings' beloved child while sound is the unruly stepchild that our brains love to hate. Compared to words (written or spoken), not only do pictures get registered in our minds quicker and stay cached in our memories for longer, we have an inherent positive bias for pictures; we tend to ignore words if they conflict with what we see.

THE MCGURK EFFECT

The McGurk Effect demonstrates beyond doubt the perceptive dominance of the visual input for the human brain over the auditory input. If a sound is paired with the visual component unrelated to that sound, we hear the sound related to the visual component rather than the original sound.

This is why communication experts and advertising consultants the world over advise advertisers to minimize the wordiness of their advertising copy and use visuals to tell strong stories. In fact this was the understanding that gave rise to info-graphics and PowerPoint decades ago. What we use PowerPoint now for, is to describe a curved line with every point equal distance from the centre. So let's admit; it's a pity how we all abused PowerPoint to regurgitate words rather than communicate real meanings through visuals. That would be a circle by the way, and sure enough; it looks like this.

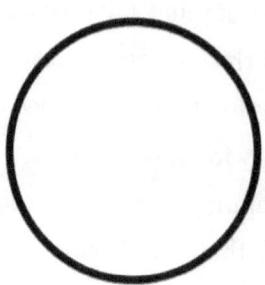

THE PICTURE SUPERIORITY EFFECT

The picture superiority effect resulted from experiments demonstrating that for recalling information from human memory, pictures do dramatically better than text. When information is presented verbally, after three days, people will only remember 10% of it. If the same information is presented visually, the human brain will recall 65% of it three days later.

This also has a broad philosophical meaning for our lives. Ralph Waldo Emerson wrote in his work "Letters and Social Aims," published in 1875:

> "Don't say things. What you are stands over you the while, and thunders so that I cannot hear what you say to the contrary. A lady of my acquaintance said, 'I don't care so much for what they say as I do for what makes them say it.'"

PAINTING MENTAL PICTURES OF OBJECTS AND EVENTS

The picture superiority effect does not suggest that you carry a pen and paper or your multimedia gizmos everywhere you go so that you could communicate with the human race, or you should forever hold your peace.

Painting mental pictures of objects and events through storytelling substitutes verbal communication for visual communication in situations where you do not have the luxury of using illustrations or pictorial representation of your verbal message. Examples, metaphors and anecdotes serve to paint a mental picture to complement the verbal content of your message.

Proposed by Allan Paivio in 1971, the Dual-coding Theory hypothesized the idea that verbal and visual representations of objects or events are coded differently by the human mind but are available alternatively to recall the object or event. Having both verbal and visual representation of the object or event in the mind complements a person's understanding of the core message and reinforces the ability of a person to recall it. When a picture and a word can do the same job that a thousand and one words would, why bother the voice cords.

THE BUSINESS LOSS OF EXCESSIVE RELIANCE ON VERBAL COMMUNICATION

Knowing what we know about the tendency of the human brain to be more respectful of the visual content vis-à-vis verbal, let's examine the top three downsides of excessive reliance on verbal communication:

1. Same words, different meanings – Depending on the social, cultural and educational background of the audience, you run the risk of communicating something contrary to what you intended to say.

2. The more the words, the lesser the ROI – Whether it is your day-to-day business communication, a board presentation or an ad campaign, excessive use of verbal communication means slower ingestion of the message into audience's memory and more time required to recall it. This means slower and less predictable call to action. Since business communication– especially advertising–is all about influencing human behaviour, use of words in place of visuals means you would end up investing more marketing dollars to influence your clients' buying behaviour. This is not because ad space for words is more expensive than for pictures, but simply because you need to spend more to put the same message across, and that translates into poor ROI. The same goes for all other forms of business communication.

3. Professional relationships go downhill at the speed of light – The tricky thing about words is, we think we are communicating what we are saying; and that's not always true. Also, since the knowledge we intend to impart through verbal communication is native to our memory, we tend to get blindsighted by our prejudice of owning the whole information. We assume that the listener already knows the preamble and we only need to tell him or her the part that is important to effect an action. What it results in is, a misinterpretation of why you intended to influence the listener's actions in the first place, and hence distrust in the nobility of your intentions. All too often, I see otherwise congenial relationships at work turning into bitterness in a matter of minutes.

* * *

Neglecting the effectiveness of complementing verbal communication with visual representation results in direct loss of business and reputation. This is simply not the kind of risk that has a proportionate return associated with it.

Ancient Egyptians used hieroglyphs instead of alphabetical symbols to communicate ideas–oftentimes complex ideas. Could it be that they knew of the picture superiority effect long before we did? Regardless of what they knew or not, with all the modern scientific evidence to suggest that we are in fact hardwired to hear with our eyes, we better start paying more attention to the incredible power of the visual.

In terms of reinventing yourself to be able to better influence people, this realization is important for two reasons.

Firstly, knowing the significant impact of the visual stimuli on human brain makes it important for us to care for our physical appearance.

Secondly, in terms of the message we communicate to people, it is crucial that we rely less on verbal content and more on visual content to transfer the meaning of the message into the minds of people as close to the original intended message as possible. If you are sure of what you want to say, you have no reason to camouflage the message in words that communicate something other than the meaning.

PART 3
Being the First Dancer

"Action is the foundational key to all success."

—Pablo Picasso

Chapter 11

The Law of Action: Your First Dance

As I said in the introduction, the first dancer doesn't wait for opportunities to knock on his doors. He finds opportunities lying inside him—waiting to be had at all times. So he does not wait for the *ideal* time to act, because he knows there is no ideal time. Time is all the same; it is the events that make it special.

The first dancer lives in the present day. He knows how to affect the events that lead to opportunities. And he has an uncanny ability to spot the opportunities that would otherwise go unnoticed for someone else. As such, the first dancer is a creator of his circumstance, not the victim of it.

He is also not too worried about the likelihood of his actions producing desirable results. He believes in his ability to act and to create change, and this belief gives him the courage to create circumstances that lead to desirable results.

As Leonardo da Vinci reportedly said,

> "It had long since come to my attention that people of accomplishment rarely sat back and let things happen to them. They went out and happened to things."

I have been quite intrigued by how these 'people of accomplishment' are able to achieve success in life while others pursuing the same goal under similar circumstances are not. It becomes more interesting when both groups of people have similar potential to achieve success. As I recounted in the story of my encounter with Mr. Victim and Mr. Creator in chapter 1, I knew deep inside that the basic differentiating factor is a set of learned attitudes.

However, a few months ago, I decided to look at the whole cause and effect pandemonium in light of the control system theory. I figured we are like electronic devices with our own built-in closed circuits taking input and producing output. Think of us as amplifiers or oscillators if you will. The output we produce is directly or inversely proportionate to the input. For instance, if you reprimand a child for doing something undesirable, he would either stop or stay on doing it with greater zeal and vigour. One way or the other, our influence will impact his action. This is the simple cause and effect relationship where the output depends on the input. We see it all around us, all the time.

Now let's get a bit more creative and think for a moment; can the output determine the input? Can we have our actions determine the influence rather than have the actions determined by the influence. This might sound simple at first. Since it is a closed loop, our actions determine the influence as much as they are determined by the influence. A favourable influence will result in a positive action, producing a stronger favourable influence and thus resulting in a stronger positive action. Notwithstanding what causes what once the cycle has started, there has to be an internal or external influence to cause the first action. Newton would call it force. I am calling it influence; same thing, different names.

A question arises then; what if the favourable influence does not exist as the starting point? What if all influences around us are negative or non-existent? In other words, if we say opportunities influence positive actions, and positive actions create positive feedback to create opportunities for more positive actions, what to do if the opportunity for that first positive action does not exist?

Do opportunities result in actions or do actions create opportunities? Does the input cause the output or does the output occur in isolation to instigate a series of input? This is the critical question that determines success in life. While I appreciate that successful people are generally good at identifying and making the most of opportunities, what largely determines success is their indifference to the existence of opportunities. Most successful people do not wait for opportunities to act. They bank on their inner grit as the only influence and work to achieve their first small success which creates an opportunity for a bigger success and thus a momentum is built. Their output creates input and intervenes throughout the flow to accentuate the strength of the input, impacting the efficacy of the output further. In terms of the control system theory, this would be loop gain.

All our favourite success stories were born this way; Steve Jobs and Mark Zuckerbergs of our times do not wait for opportunities. When they first set off working on their idea from their garages, they have no clear opportunities in sight and no clue if they would ever come by. They don't have the CEOs of major Silicon Valley VC firms lined up at their doors. Their actions create opportunities. With due respect to Sir Isaac Newton, it appears that the first law of motion does not hold true when it comes to these first dancers.

As you would recall, the law states that an object at rest tends to stay at rest and that an object in uniform motion tends to stay in uniform motion unless acted upon by a net external force. The thing is, first dancers do not wait for a net external force acting upon them; neither does the continuation of their action rely on a constant intervention of an external force. Their action happens in absence of (and creates) an external force.

To me, seven things are the hallmark of a first dancer. If you do the following, the law of action works to bring about success whether or not there is an opportunity to achieve success. In many ways, these seven elements summarize the true character of the first dancer and helps him be the first among equals and attract unlimited opportunities.

1. CREATE A PERCEPTION OF SUCCESS

People would want to lend their attention to you, and invest time and money in you only if they see potential in you. The most compelling evidence of potential is past success. If they do not get a constant supply of successes to reaffirm their belief that you are successful, they will stop right there. With no continuous motion, the force that has been intensifying the motion will die out.

To create opportunities out of thin air, you have to create success first. But then, if you think your success can not arise in absence of an opportunity, why not create a 'perception of success' to lure opportunities? You have to start the positive feedback loop somewhere.

In your own mind, think of yourself as successful. Dress, walk and talk like successful people do. As much as you can while staying within your means and not coming across as a narcissistic egomaniac, embrace the lifestyle of success. Do it in a positive, socially conscientious way. Help people, share your knowledge with them, guide them to success, and encourage them to positivity. You will feel successful and that feeling will resonate with those around you, taking in its cheerful embrace all the opportunities that once seemed out of sight.

2. DON'T WAIT FOR LUCK

I always thought that the shortest distance between failure and success is luck. It so appears now that if you account for the wait time, the shortest distance between failure and success is action. Acting now is crucial. If you want to be financially successful, pay off that credit card bill now even if that means using up every spare penny you have. If you want to be regarded as an opinion leader, write that first article or go make that first presentation now. The time would never be right to take the plunge. Hang on and don't react to your fight-or-flight impulse; do the contrary, especially when it comes to flight.

It is not to say you would be successful the first time you take that leap of faith; quite the opposite in fact—you are more likely to fail than to succeed. But fail now to be successful later, rather than wait a lifetime for the right opportunity to act. If you play your cards right, you should be done with all your failures before you turn 30 and have the taste of your first success while you still have time to enjoy the perks of it.

All too often, we underestimate how uncontrollable time is, until it's too late to fail. When we are young, we are either too busy taking the wrong kinds of risks or taking no risks at all. You have to make a conscious decision to reach for higher goals compared to your peers. It takes an incredible amount of courage and tenacity to knowingly reach for goals that test your talents and your will to succeed. But again, better do that sooner than later.

3. TAKE BABY STEPS

If you don't have an opportunity to begin with, start with tiny successes. Your first small success will lead you to an opportunity to achieve bigger success and the positive feedback loop will come alive. We all have those little moments to shine and to make a difference. Take all your elevator speeches, your time out with your boss, your class reunions, your savings and your good health as opportunities to achieve those little successes.

Plan only as much as you need to achieve that first little success. Do keep your vision of the future intact, but don't be overwhelmed by all that it takes to reach there in the next five or ten years. Focus on what you can achieve today or this week that will eventually lead you to that bigger success.

4. DON'T CARE ABOUT GETTING IT RIGHT THE FIRST TIME

Who said you ought to get it right the first time, every time? Life isn't a fairytale or a Nikon ad campaign. When it comes to learning success, action is your school, and failure your teacher. Try and get along with your teacher if you wish to graduate from the school of action into the real life of success.

Failure is not a cause for shame; it is a step in the right direction. It is the path to the destination. How can you just skip the path and land right at the destination? The sooner you set out on that journey the sooner you will reach there. The fact is, your life starts all over again, the moment you realize failure is progress.

5. HAVE THE ATTITUDE FOR SUCCESS

Let's be real. There is no net external force out there that cares enough to make you successful. However there is an internal force in us all and it emanates from self-awareness. Call it your ambition, your will to succeed or your drive to be persistent. No matter what you call it, it is this internal force that shapes up your attitude for success. And your attitude for success is what creates your disregard for the existence of opportunities and your reliance on action. Not only that, the positivity of your attitude attracts like-minded people to you and that creates opportunities for continuation of your action.

6. BE WILLING TO OUTSTRETCH

Challenging yourself does not always have to be about trying out unachievable feats. Dream big but cherish small achievements that require you to outstretch beyond your known potential at present. As you grow, how much you can outstretch will grow with it.

Anyone can come up with big ideas, but not too many are willing to do what it takes to implement small ideas. Remember all the famous people who made others' ideas possible? You just have to challenge yourself to do something that is achievable but has an element of outstretch to it too.

Your learning along the way will prepare you for bigger challenges, way beyond your known potential. Your potential can still be limited. You don't need to be a genius. All geniuses are not successful just like all successful people are not geniuses. You'd rather be successful than a genius.

7. BE THANKFUL FOR OPPORTUNITIES

When your actions create opportunities, be thankful to those who acknowledged your positive actions and provided you with greater opportunities. It serves to multiply your opportunities further. When you show gratitude, it is not just your action creating opportunities but your thankfulness as well. It is almost miraculous how action and gratitude can join forces to manufacture success for you even when the odds seem against you at first.

    To me, this is the law of action; beyond repudiation. I have seen far too many examples to disregard this as something less than a law of nature. When you set your eyes on a goal and work persistently to achieve it, your first action is not necessarily proportionate to the success it creates, it hardly ever is. It takes time to generate the inertia that creates a success proportionate to the action, or even go beyond that to create a success far bigger than your action. So when it comes to human success, I'm pretty sure the object doesn't need a net external force to move it.

Chapter 12

Live to Give:
Your Legacy Will Outlive Your Fame

To become the first among equals and to attract unlimited opportunities in life, you have to be a giver—someone the world would look up to. Your value in society is not determined by what you get from it, but by what you give back to it. I learned this by chance one day.

What I witnessed at a Toronto subway station on a busy Saturday afternoon transformed my views on giving for good. I was right behind a young couple in the line at the ticketing booth and was already hypnotized by the enchanting innocence of their five-year old daughter who had all eyes affixed on her. As her parents handed her some loose change encouraging her to pay for her own ticket, she suddenly jumped out of the line and ran to put the coins in the black tray placed in front of a miserable-looking old man playing what looked like a bluegrass banjo. People couldn't but turn their heads to notice that unquestionably selfless gesture of giving; unquestionable because there could have been nothing else in the little child's mind other than the pure joy of giving.

She ran back to her father with open arms and hugged him tightly in anticipation of his fervent appreciation for accomplishing a great feat of valour. As some men and women walked up to the parents with broad smiles on their faces and shook their hands, I'm sure the little angel got more appreciation than she had ever hoped for. I saw a sparkle in her bright blue eyes that I cannot forget in a hundred years.

Minutes later, I felt as if this had turned something on in me. While sitting in the train, my mind intuitively drifted to weave stories around what this might mean for the next few hours or days in the lives of the people who witnessed it.

The old man for example would stop by at that small bakery outside the station and buy some croissants for the people he shares the shelter with. That would be quite a treat for the dejected old souls at the shelter, perhaps resurrecting in their feeble hearts the pleasures of the lost times they thought had deserted them; much like their loved ones.

Or that well-dressed middle-aged lady who was the first person to congratulate the proud parents on having raised a humane soul amid the quagmire of greed and antagonism that this world has become. Perhaps she would reassess the bitterness of her gratuitous agitation on the phone only five minutes back on someone's decision to marry a person she didn't approve of. If it was her daughter she was talking about, she would call her the same evening and let her know that she will always be there to support her decision and to cherish the bliss of finding the love of her life.

The life of the curly-haired man would take a turn for good too. He would finally make the call that his father had been waiting many years for. He would find the courage to apologize for his callousness on the day he left his parents' home seven years ago to follow his dreams–the dreams he could never find. He would tell him that spending all those years running after a mirage of love for the things and people he thought would comfort his soul, had in fact emptied his soul of whatever goodness it had in it to begin with–the goodness his father had ever so lovingly inculcated in his heart while he was growing up in a small town.

I haven't forgotten about that alluringly beautiful girl who waited for the people to disperse so that she could bend on her knees with teary eyes and kiss the young child's blushing cheeks. The way she looked into the little girl's eyes and how the kid blithely responded to the warmth of her look made me think that she could see herself as a child in the little one's benevolent eyes. I did not know what her story was. Maybe she was new in town and had no one to turn to as she struggled to establish herself and make a respectable living. I have lesser idea of what she would do to pay it forward. But looking at her convinced me that she would make a lasting impact in people's lives with the compassion and gentleness that overflowed from her eyes one drop at a time.

I learned something that day. I knew that learning happens by chance. For real learning, one has to accept the challenges that come with it. Taking up the challenges that life throws your way and being willing to step out of your comfort zone is the only way to learn something that would last a lifetime. Learning opportunities that are easier to come by are easier to go by unnoticed.

It is only by accepting challenges that we truly expand the canvas of personal development. Taking, hoarding and squandering are much closer to human nature than giving. Still, only when the impulse of giving takes over does one get the true joy he was originally seeking through the triad. That is right—we get something by giving. And what we get is what we all knowingly or unknowingly have been searching for—a legacy to be proud of. It is very practical then to create a giving chain and draw the joy of giving from every action we take.

If we touch someone's heart today with just one deed of kindness, one by one, our lives, our families, our communities, and the world at large would become dynamos of change. It would take time for the first push to give way to a sustained momentum, but with every new link added to the chain, a multitude of new links will be created and the network would grow to take over the whole world. However idealistic it may sound, this is our only hope and our only chance.

At an individual level, you long for the enigmatic charm of giving when you have had the first glimpse of the light. And then you are uncontrollably lured to bathe in the enlightening rays of your new-found sun—to rejoice in the infinite warmth that sets you free from the capitalistic impulses and the growing pains of following your dreams.

* * *

I read a wonderful article by Bob Patton on the true meaning of human legacy. Bob's inspiring story about his father-in-law instantly reminded me of my mother's uncle who for many years has been an inspiration for me and many others I've known.

His life's work is not fully represented by the professional stature that he rose to as the President of one of the biggest global financial institutions of the world, but by the innumerable souls that his most humble and compassionate acts of kindness touched. Reflecting on his unwavering strength of character has provided me solace in the toughest of times. I always heard him say that the true measure of an individual's character is how he treats a person who cannot do any good to him. Through his selfless devotion to the good of humanity, he brought to life the profoundness of the adage:

> *"Carve your name on hearts, not tombstones. A legacy is etched into the minds of others and the stories they share about you."*

A few years ago, when I was working for a large bank in Pakistan, I got a call from one of my Regional Sales Managers one afternoon, requesting my availability for a meeting with a high-net-worth client. I asked for the intent of the meeting and agreed to meet the client although given the level of delegation prevalent in the organization, I seldom needed to meet with clients personally.

The next morning, I looked through the glass wall of my office to see the gentleman in his late 50's, gracefully attired in a glen plaid flannel suit slowly walking up to my office with a walking stick tightly gripped in his hand. As he entered the office, accompanied by one of my colleagues, I stood up to greet him and we sat down to talk. We hardly talked for five minutes before I decided to sign his request concerning his mortgage with the bank. We then moved to talk about the state of the banking business and the economy in general. The conversation soon turned to the particular bank which was headed by my mother's uncle until only a few years back.

The gentleman reminisced his good times as the bank's client. He explained how the world used to be a better place when institutions were run by self-effacing, gracious and kindhearted men and women with the underlying vision to promote a human cause.

He then went on to tell me a story concerning my mother's uncle without knowing my relationship with him. He told me about the many people who applied for work at the bank despite not having the requisite qualifications or experience. Job applications from talented but financially less privileged candidates that would make it to the President's desk were seldom rejected.

Surprised at this, I asked him why the President would allow hiring an unqualified employee. His voice started to crack and tears appeared to roll down his old wrinkled cheeks as he responded. I could not have been less prepared to handle an elderly sniveling gentleman in my office on a fine Tuesday morning. Extending a tissue box across the table to him, I quickly glanced through the glass wall to make sure this anomalous situation wasn't attracting any unwanted attention outside in the hall.

He took a pause, smiled and said, "He wouldn't keep them on the bank's payroll but pay their salaries from his personal account and let them upgrade their education while getting practical experience at the bank. He had been doing that for years and had made the necessary arrangements so that they would never know who paid their salaries. Consider it an unpaid internship for the bank's official purpose."

Completely astonished by what I had just heard, I found myself unable to speak for a moment. He continued, "I am privy to this inside scoop due to my father's friendship with the bank's President. He had hundreds of people getting their salaries right out of his investment income without anyone but only the very close friends knowing about it." All his philanthropic work and the enormous charitable funds he had founded (that the public knew about), comprised only a fraction of his selfless acts of giving at a personal level.

I attempted to contemplate what that would have meant for the beneficiaries. I could picture this one individual being the sole reason for hundreds of families getting their livelihood, being able to send their children to schools, providing for their aging parents and doing all this without a shard of damage to their dignity.

I shook the gentleman's hand and thanked him for sharing one of life's most meaningful lessons with me. As he got ready to leave, I thought for a moment that I should let him know that I am related to the person he so greatly revered, but decided against it. After he had left, I sat at my desk feeling deeply moved by what I'd been told. There are people in our midst who choose to bequeath *values* and not *valuables* to the world as their legacy. What's more, they don't care about getting anything in return. In fact they do whatever is necessary to stay behind the scenes.

I understood that day how true human legacy outlives personal fame. Throughout our lives, we strive to be known for our success. We get famous for what we achieve in life; everything that we own—our wealth, our education, our professional titles and our accomplishments. Still, what we fail to realize is that these things are an integral part of our mortal selves; when we die, our fame dies with it. What lives on is how we made others feel, how we treated the people around us and how we made their lives better.

It is the story that a parent passes on to the child that lives on. It is what you create for the world and not what you acquire for yourself that lasts. If we try to use the latter to achieve the former, we leave a legacy behind long after our fame has disintegrated into memories. Legacy is not a memory; it is your life's story–living and breathing like a pulsating heart. It is the change you bring about in this world.

In Bob's words, "Legacy is built by living your values consistently on a daily basis." Legacy is making the world a better place with your character, helping one person at a time. Everyone has a story; everyone has a legacy. Our legacy reflects our understanding of the life's purpose. If only we had the courage to ask ourselves how we would like to be remembered, we could take control of our own story to build a lasting legacy.

Chapter 13

Economic Freedom: Challenging the Norms

I mentioned in the last chapter that the human society values a person not based on what he or she has, but what he or she could give back to the society. Today, we respect (or pretend to respect) the wealthy and the powerful not because of what they have accomplished for themselves, but because of what we hope and expect their wealth and their position could mean for us.

Take a plunge into the mind of a die-hard fan of a Hollywood celebrity and you will find the same thought process. The reason a fan would be willing to do anything to have a photo op with the celebrity is not because of the fame, the wealth or the social status the celebrity enjoys per se, but because of what the photo will mean for the fan. To be associated with an accomplished actor would give immense satisfaction to the fan that he would cherish a lifetime. It is this satisfaction that the fan is looking for.

Could this fan's satisfaction be shared with other fans the same way he derived satisfaction from being associated with the celebrity's fame through a photo op? Could he just distribute small gift boxes full of chunks of his satisfaction to other fans? I seriously doubt that would be possible.

Much the same way, people will be attracted towards you if they see value in the interaction. In chapter 6, I called this 'promise of value' that you build through personal branding. This value is communicated in many ways—both subtle and explicit.

It is not enough to know that the world around you is attracted to you only when you have something to offer to the world; it is also important to know what it takes to create that promise of value. A philanthropic billionaire would not have been able to help people through his wealth had he not worked to earn that wealth in the first place. The abundant satisfaction he gets from the honourable work he does would not have been possible if he had not worked hard to create his first business. Economic freedom is therefore the underpinning for a life of abundance.

Let's pause here for a moment and let me share something with you. What you will read next is an MBA's last resignation letter. In fact, it is more than a resignation letter. If you pay attention to what is said between the lines, you would feel that is typifies the story of every working class man and woman.

Dear Boss,

I write this letter today to tell you that I lied to you.

Yes, you heard me right. Not once, not twice, but every day since the last 11 years that I've been working here, I lied to you. In every nuance of my voice and in every gesture of my body, I lied.

Still, I did not consider myself guilty of deceit. That is so because I lied to myself too. And my lies were so convincing that I actually thought I was telling everyone only the truth. I have been lying since my first day at work many years ago; not only to you but to all the bosses I have had in the past 19 years. It flowed in my veins and nourished my ravenous desire to have a successful career; I never suspected myself of lying for even a second.

But what happened last night has flustered my conscience to a degree irreparable by any amount of commiseration or any false promise of success. As I turned back to leave my 10 year old son's room after putting him to bed, I heard his meek whisper, "daddy, can I say something to you?" I immediately walked back to him and stood right next to his bed, "sure my angel, what do you want to say?"

"I am proud of you dad," he said. "I am proud of you for being the youngest VP in your entire company and for achieving so many awards for your work." I listened carefully in anticipation of a deeper message to follow as I noticed his starry little eyes looking straight into my tired soulless eyes. He went on, "but daddy, I would be prouder if you were as happy as you used to be before you got so busy." I patted his head and walked out of the room.

Back in my bed, I called to mind how my father could not afford to send me to school and how he had to sell his car to pay my semester fees when I had joined college. I remembered how he used to console my mother by saying that everything would be fine once I started to make a living for myself. All I needed was an MBA and our world would turn into a Utopian paradise of progress and prosperity. How grounded I thought our hopes and aspirations were.

While I lay there, all my years at work flashed right in front of my eyes. I saw myself staying back at work one night to finish a report that the CEO was to present to the directors next day. I missed my son's seventh birthday that day and came back home to see a piece of cake on the dining table with a handwritten note from him saying, "Dad, I wish you were here tonight." I also recalled the day I left with a delegation to China after I had volunteered in place of a colleague who had taken a couple of days off to attend his mother's funeral. The next day my son was to be given the 'best student of the year' award in an extravagant ceremony at school.

As I write this letter to you so leisurely sitting here at home this morning, I recall how rushed my mornings always have been. I never had enough time to have a decent breakfast, or sometimes, a breakfast at all. I recall how I was always getting late for something or the other. Still, I always used to think to myself, what if I could not make this world a Utopian paradise of prosperity for my parents who breathed their last without giving up their unwavering trust in my commitment to my career. A generation lost is a generation saved, I thought.

Then my mind drifted to recollect the tedious lessons I learned in business school; how the ultimate goal of an enterprise is to maximize profit and how professionals like us work to steer the economy forward, contributing our remarkable wisdom to create jobs and propel the wheel of holy capitalism. Things like ROI, opportunity cost, SWOT and efficiency of production crossed my mind.

I then paused to reflect on my position in this whole quagmire of hawkish competition and insatiable combative lust for money and power. I thought to myself "who have I been working for?" Certainly not for myself, or for my dead parents, or for my family. What about my ROI and my opportunity cost? More importantly, what about my happiness and my son's pride? I thought and thought and thought.

This morning, as I write this letter to you, I feel the wisdom of my son's innocuous expression weigh heavier than all of the thick books I had studied at business school. All the missed opportunities of spending time with him as he was growing up, all those missed breakfasts and wedding anniversaries, each of my projects' milestones that distracted me from appreciating my life's significant landmarks as I rushed past them towards the Utopia my father had dreamed of for me, had made me an unhappier person. And the irony is—I have been lying to myself and to you whenever I said or implied that this was my dream, my passion, my life's work. I was programmed from an early age to ignore my inner calling and misinterpret life and the meaning of success. I had been fooled to think that making the rich richer with your sweat and blood keeps you happy. Career success and making a living off fixed salary is the holy grail of success in the modern corporatized world of Orwellian wellbeing. The truth is; I lied.

As much as I had convinced myself that I was living the dream, the truth is that I had only been dying to live. It wasn't my dream to let my employers work my tail off so that they could get away with all the profit I worked to earn for them. I sneered at the concept of work-life-balance because I was brainwashed into believing that my sacrifice amounts to something. I thought of myself as a significant member of the elite power that makes the world go round. I lied to you because I was lied to.

I know you would be in awe, thinking how I was able to achieve such enviable professional success if this wasn't even my dream. The truth is; I don't know how. Perhaps being lied to made me capable of achieving this mirage of success. Imagine then, what chasing the truth would have made me capable of achieving. My dream was to have a small business of my own, to see it grow and to cherish the fruits of my own labour. That was my dream.

The brightness of my son's eyes tells me that all is not lost. He will fulfill his dream. I will not let him be lied to. I will help him find the truth that the book of life would teach him, not the textbooks. He will learn the concepts of ROI, opportunity cost, profit maximization and risk management as they apply to human lives, not corporations. He will live his dream, and mine too. He will not die to live but to live and be happy for the choices he made.

Please accept my resignation as I have accepted another job, working for the good of myself and my family. Starting today, I will live on my own terms, not fearing those who have had the absolute power to disparage me all my life. This is not my resignation only to you but also to the entire world system that has made us humans mere slaves of the whims of the haves.

Sincerely,

Employee

I wrote this letter to share the perspective of a dear friend who passed away a few months ago. It was always enlightening to hear his atypical views on the flip side of business and life in general. He lived his life as an average white collar guy singularly focused on making ends meet for himself and his family. People expected his views to reflect the mediocrity of his life. However, it was only after I had a chance to get to know him for what he truly was that I discovered his rebellious alter ego that has fascinated me to this day. Whenever I asked him why he lived a life that did not reflect his views about the world, his reply would always start with "only if." Based on my understanding of his lens for looking at things, he would have written this resignation letter if he'd ever gotten a chance to–only if.

He was a common man who played it safe all his life. Not doing anything crazy that would jeopardize his stable salary and would let his wife and his kids down. He played safe just like we all do, dreaming of a life other than the one we have but too afraid to do what is necessary to change our life.

Einstein is thought to have said, "Everybody is a genius. But if you judge a fish by its ability to climb a tree, it will live its whole life believing that it is stupid." Too often we see that people end up in vocations they are not meant to be in. It wouldn't be surprising if you loved art in school but ended up becoming an accountant. The fish might be able to climb the tree if it was taught to, but it would still be a fish. This would be extremely unfortunate.

The dilemma of our times is that too many of us are holding on to jobs we were never meant to do, but fear the alternative worse. As Charles Bukowksi said:

> *"We become bodies with fearful and obedient minds. The color leaves the eye. The voice becomes ugly. And the body. The hair. The fingernails. The shoes. Everything does."*

We become the fish that struggles to climb the tree but never gets to swim. We are fish out of water, and expected to compete against monkeys and squirrels, as well as poor turtles and penguins, too afraid to admit that we were never meant to climb trees, because that fear is what keeps us alive; barely alive.

Freedom is an expensive commodity, and the thought of revolt; paralyzingly terrifying. It is a thought that we would not want to enter our minds. The fear of being laid off from work is greater than the fear of wasting one's entire life doing what one wasn't meant to. Such is the ironic truth of our times. And since all monkeys, squirrels, turtles, penguins and fish are expected to climb trees and be all the same at it, they are judged by their ability to climb trees. An accountant does not have to be an artist at heart; too bad he was born one.

Yet, not putting one's genius to use, not enduring the pains of revolt and giving up your right to achieve the excellence you were destined to achieve is like betraying nature. It is like being thankless for the most valuable gift you have been given.

Most of us choose to ignore the inner voice that tells us to be the best at something, only because we are good enough at something else. Then there are those who do not let their success come in the way of their excellence. Their fear of having wasted an entire life is greater than the fear of not being able to make a living and put food on the table. Who would you rather be?

***

Economic freedom comes at a cost. When you find yourself stuck in the rut, doing more of the same thing that got you stuck in that place will not get you out of it. The cost of economic freedom is a paradigm shift in your mindset. You have to question the assumptions that determine your market value, the norms that define the distribution of wealth, and the models that establish economic hierarchies. You have to be willing to question everything you have known to be true your entire life.

Your employer will tell you that the monetary value of your skills, your education and your experience is a certain dollar amount. They will determine your worth by a yardstick of their own making. They will tell you the acceptable salary range for the position you applied for. And that sounds fair.

That sounds fair until you realize that your skills, education and experience are not the only determinants of your potential. Your human potential goes way beyond what your transcripts tell you, or the number of years that quantify your experience. How do you know your potential can be measured by a certain dollar amount? Who said your earning potential is $50,000 or $100,000? Why can't it be $1,000,000 or $10,000,000?

Until you take back the right to determine your own financial worth, you will not be able to achieve economic freedom. Your income potential should not be limited by the 'average salary range' for your position. It should not be limited by *anything* other than your imagination. You are not average; why should your income be? But as long as your capacity to earn money is measured by the number of hours you spend working, your income potential will remain limited. The next chapter looks at the shift in mindset necessary to break the limits.

This is not a book on personal financial management. It will not tell you how to get rich quickly. But it will set you up for financial freedom by opening up your mind to infinite possibilities to achieve success. More than your actions, your mental framework will determine if you are able to embark on a journey to economic freedom and live a life of abundance.

Based on the foundation built in this chapter, the next chapter will provide a framework of the mindset you need to develop in order to understand and achieve financial independence. Achieving this independence is not possible without challenging the norms of the economic system in your mind; it is also not possible without converting your millionaire mindset into actionable steps that would form your financial habits over the long run. Therefore, the next chapter is crucial if you want to learn about achieving financial independence.

Chapter 14

The Millionaire Mind: Thinking Rich

I named this chapter after Dr. Thomas J. Stanley's famous book, "The Millionaire Mind," first published in 2000. Stanley's book does not pander to people's desires to hit the jackpot. It does not blabber about the trivia of financial technicalities and meaningless jargon; it presents vivid sketches of first-generation millionaires and exemplifies key differences between the "Income Sheet Affluent" and the "Balance Sheet Affluent" millionaires—differences in terms of their mindsets as well as their lifestyles.

Before we begin, it is extremely critical to fully understand two things. Firstly, it is never impossible to get out of any financial challenges you might be in. Do not think that financial difficulties are ordained upon you, or that you are not meant to be rich. If people with much less intelligence than you can amass stupendous amounts of wealth, so can you.

Secondly, it is not a particular financial strategy that would help you achieve wealth; but a mindset—a lifestyle. While strategies are time-bound and change with respect to circumstances, the mindset is an enduring characteristic of a person. It determines your attitude towards money thus giving it a high degree of permanence. If your attitude towards money and the resulting behaviour emanate from the millionaire mind, they would set you on the trajectory to become financially independent.

YOU CONTROL THE MONEY; MONEY DOESN'T CONTROL YOU

The first mindset change is to recognize that money should not have the power to control you. Remember that money is a tool to attain material wealth. It is a means to an end. Material wealth in turn, makes people happy. It would make you feel good if you had a beautiful house and shiny expensive cars. This might sound obvious but I need you to internalize the thought.

If we know that material wealth makes us happy and the way to get material wealth is only through money, how do you get the money? There are only two ways you can have money. You either borrow the money, or you earn it. One might argue that since you end up getting the money either way, there's not much difference as long as it gets you the material wealth you sought. Once you buy that house or those shiny cars regardless of how you get them, you'll be happy.

Let me ask you then; can money buy happiness? Well, looking at the hundreds of rich people I have met as a banker over the past many years, my reply would be an emphatic 'yes.' But don't be surprised. Bear with me.

It is understandable that a millionaire may be happy, but an ordinary person might be content. Whatever way you get your hands on that money, as long as it gets you the material wealth, it will make you happy. But for you to be content, the money used to achieve material wealth should meet certain criteria—in terms of both where it comes from and where it goes. Money leads to happiness while financial independence leads to contentment.

This is the universal truth about human mind. It does not differ from person to person. Contentment is not happiness. Depending on the method and the circumstance in which it is acquired, money can not only bring you happiness but contentment too. However, it is important to be absolutely sure what you are looking for. I will explain that further in chapter 15 of this book, but for now let's stick to money matters.

As I said, money is a tool. Just like any other tool, you use money to do something. The tool doesn't use you; you use the tool. You can either let money determine your actions or you can take control of your actions and let them determine your financial future. As we established in the last chapter, you have to challenge the norms that put a price on your potential in terms of averages. Once you realize that your financial potential is virtually limitless and build the confidence to position yourself to maximize that potential, your changed attitude towards money attracts opportunities that seemed out of sight.

However, be mindful that letting money control your actions could be a pitfall. The mindset that allows money to control our decisions gives rise to an attitude that considers the society (friends, family and community) merely the means to acquire financial wealth. This attitude gives rise to actions that are singularly focused on becoming rich. Ironically, these actions seldom bear fruit.

We have countless examples of people around us to prove this. All those living a seemingly luxurious life on their credit cards let money determine their actions and are never able to build real wealth. Conversely, we see those who used their meagre incomes to build assets worth millions of dollars. Why this contrast? Simply put, the latter group controlled money while the former let money control them. To better grasp this idea, it is important to understand what financial independence really means.

WHAT IS FINANCIAL INDEPENDENCE?

I asked this question at a workshop, and invariably everyone in the audience said financial independence is having enough money to fulfill all your desires. Unfortunately, that answer is the product of the mindset we have unknowingly developed through our exposure to the popular media over the last many decades.

Financial independence is not about having lots of money. It is about *not being dependent* on others for your needs; whether it's your employer, your parents or your lender. A person with a monthly household expenditure of $25,000 with enough means to cover it month after month is not necessarily independent if he depends excessively on credit or on his active employment to generate enough cash. He might even be in a negative cash flow situation and need to work extra hours to generate the extra income he needs to sustain his household expenses and lifestyle. Financial independence is about having your money work for you; not you having to work for the money.

A good example of a financially independent person would be Santonio, the owner of the small corner shop a block away from my office. Over the past months, I got to know a lot about Santonio's mindset about money and his personal lifestyle. He does not earn enough to sustain a monthly household expenditure of $25,000 but then he doesn't 'need' that kind of money to maintain a good lifestyle. In his mid-fifties now, Santonio has no credit (except supplier's credit limit); he has his mortgage fully paid off and drives a 6-year old Toyota Corolla that he bought on cash. He saves over 40% of his income and invests in rental real estate. The rent he generates from the properties he owns goes into another bank account, from where it is partly invested in medium-risk liquid securities. He has enough savings to not only pay for his daughter's university education but also his grandchildren's. He takes vacation every year and lives in a good neighbourhood.

Santonio is financially independent, and he's not only happy but content too. I'm sure he is not bemused at the end of every month looking at his credit card bills, worrying how to settle them only to get on with another consumption frenzy next month. His contentment and equanimity are not only palpable, they are contagious. To me, Santonio exemplifies the mindset of the financially independent.

DON'T DEPEND ON CREDIT

Truth be told. As a career banker, I've never been too excited to see my credit card portfolio earning subpar interest income. Providing free credit to poor households has never been the intent behind launching credit cards. In fact, I would use every marketing strategy in the book to lure cardholders to overspend and get into the interest paying cycle.

A critical element of financial independence is not depending on credit cards. Personally, I am not too fond of having large credit card limits. If I can't pay 100% of the credit limit in a month, it is too much for my need. People say they keep credit cards so that they could pay for high-ticket purchases without needing to use their own money. Well, if you can't afford to buy a new television with your own cash, you probably shouldn't. Besides, what does your cash do sitting in a chequing account anyway?

Similarly, if your predictable expenses like monthly grocery are paid for with your credit card, you are actually taking credit for your basic consumption needs. The only reason someone would do that is if the $2,000 cash he would have spent on grocery was yielding him enormous profits, which is highly unlikely. If you think it is wise to use someone else's money for your basic needs, wait till you end up using your own money for someone else's needs. That's what us bankers live for.

It is more important to know how the human mind works than to know how money works. Consumer behaviour is not determined by math but psychology. Credit card business feeds off our feelings of fear, social anxiety and greed. You fear that if you use your own money to buy that television, you wouldn't have enough left at the end of the month for basic sustenance needs. When you see your brother-in-law showing off his new $3,500 Giorgio Armani suit, you hide your anxiety behind your wry smile. Or when you see an expensive golf set and have the option to pay with credit card, you don't mind paying a premium. Having these feelings indicates that there is strong likelihood that you will end up utilizing the credit limit beyond your repayment capacity because over time you will have convinced yourself that your needs are beyond your means.

Robyn M. Dawes, a famous psychologist who specialized in the field of human judgment challenged through his research the idea that humans are rational actors. Following his work in 1976, many researchers asserted a need to move away from the notion that human judgment is a product of a rational decision making process, to a view that it is in fact based on heuristics and shortcuts. This idea was further corroborated by Shelly E. Taylor, an eminent professor of psychology at the University of California, Los Angeles, when she characterized human actions as dependent on judgments and decisions based on "scant data, which are seemingly haphazardly combined and influenced by preconceptions."

These preconceptions are ingrained in the minds of unsuspecting consumers through marketing messages that use psychological manipulations to lure customers to get credit. Not only that; the use of language and imagery is aimed at encouraging consumers to increase credit card limits beyond their buying power. The consumer goes around flaunting his credit limit to his friends and family as an evidence of his financial success. Once he has obtained credit and a high credit limit, it is time now to tempt him to use the entire limit through attractive 'deals' that would ensnare him in the vicious cycle of minimum payments.

A consumer whose monthly repayment capacity is $400 (with other bills to pay too), would have hard time paying off a $5,000 credit card debt accumulated over a few months. As a result, he would start making minimum payments just to keep his credit score from taking a nosedive. In doing so, he would be paying exorbitant interest rates on the outstanding balance. With no means to increase his monthly cash flow, his only answer to the predicament would be to get a line of credit or a loan consolidation product—another debt to pay off the original debt.

Every dollar paid in interest takes away a dollar from your potential savings. These savings could have been invested in profitable avenues to provide you a stable income as well as a financial safety net. In time, this would have made you financially independent.

USING YOUR INCOME STATEMENT TO BUILD YOUR BALANCE SHEET

You use your balance sheet to achieve financial independence, not your income statement. The primary purpose of your income statement is to build a strong balance sheet. Any income that is in excess of your monthly expenditure goes into your balance sheet. If you don't have any excess income at present, refer to the section in this chapter on creating multiple sources of income by monetizing time.

Just like anything in life, building a balance sheet takes patience. You have to live well below your means. Every time you feel the urge to spend, ask yourself the following three questions:

1. Do I *really* want it?
2. Do I *need* it?
3. Do I need it *right now*?

If the answer to any of these questions is 'no' make no effort to justify the purchase in your head. Every cent saved is a cent earned in your income statement and will go into your balance sheet as retained cash.

Someone I have known for many years has an interesting way of making sure she is working towards building her balance sheet. At the start of every year, she creates a balance sheet for the next 12 months. She writes down the assets and the liabilities she would have by the end of the year, starting with what she owns and owes today. This gives her a goal to work on. The idea is simply to increase your income generating assets and reduce your income depleting liabilities every year so that you are able to reduce dependence of your monthly income. Come next year, you repeat the same process.

UNDERSTANDING TYPES OF INCOME

We depend on money for basic sustenance. We all assume that to earn money we have to work. While that is partly correct, working for money is not the only way to earn money. That is just one kind of income—earned income.

Let's take a step back. What is it that you really do when you work to earn a salary? What are you exactly doing when you wake up every morning, put nice clothes on, drive to work, juggle multiple priorities and work your ass off to meet impossible deadlines? What you are really doing is using your *human capital* to produce *income*.

You are using your intelligence, your health, your education and training, your creativity, your experience and your skills to produce income for an organization. You take a part of that income away each month as your salary. Most of us believe that this is the only way to earn money—using our human capital to generate income. Since actively using human capital is our only perceived source of income, we assume that all our expenses will come out of this income. That is the single most glaring financial mistake we all commit.

Using our human capital is just one way to earn money; it is not the only way. In terms of classical economics, there are three primary factors of production—land, labour and capital. Using your human capital is just one of the three factors—the *labour*. So what are the other ways to earn money? The other two ways are to use your land and capital to generate income; these incomes are called *passive* and *portfolio* incomes respectively.

1. Earned income – *using labour*
2. Passive income – *using land*
3. Portfolio income – *using capital*

In order to achieve financial independence, you have to diversify your sources of income. You have to de-risk your total income from each individual factor that generates it. For example, your earned income depends on *what you do*, which in turn is a factor of *who you are*—how intelligent you are, how healthy you are, how skillful you are, how educated you are etc. De-risking your total income would mean depending less on what you are to earn your total income.

That would mean, spreading the risk across other two income sources—the ones that depend on *what you have*. If you have a real estate that generates you an income through rent for example, you will continue generating income whether or not you retain your health. Your income will no longer depend on who you are or how much you work. This is called passive income.

In the same way, when you put your money to work and generate more money, you are generating portfolio income. Your capital is the factor of production creating income for you. Examples of portfolio income would be your dividend income or your interest income on your fixed savings.

The idea is to reduce dependence on earned income as time goes by, so that your land and your money work to create income for you while you do not have to use your health, intelligence, skills, education and experience to generate money. Instead, you put these precious resources to better use. You do things that really matter, like spending time with your family, traveling around the world, writing a book or building a charity. Once the bulk of your total income starts coming from passive and portfolio sources, you can spend your time doing things that you really love to do and get your earned income from that work. No wonder a public speaker going around the world delivering lectures does not have to worry about the next project deadline or the next monthly closing. He has the time needed to do what he has passion for. He does not live to earn money; he maximizes his human capital to do things that matter more.

I see people focused so much on maximizing earned income that the thought of doing what it takes to create the other two types of income doesn't even cross their minds. If they are not satisfied with their current salary, all they can think of is working harder for the next promotion, switching jobs, upgrading their skill set through training or getting a diploma or certification. That is so because while they might be aware of the other two sources of income, they consider them out of reach. They think that earning passive income and portfolio income is something for the rich guys, not for the ordinary folks like them.

That is nothing but a fallacy. What they are forgetting is that there is one other resource they have which they aren't converting to money at present. Once they start using that resource to expand their earned income, they would have the capital needed to invest in passive and portfolio income sources. That resource is called *time*.

CREATING MULTIPLE INCOME SOURCES BY MONETIZING TIME

Almost three years ago, I met a couple who was struggling financially and was visibly depressed by the situation. Joyce, who had a diploma in graphics design, was a receptionist working at a seniors centre in Richmond Hill and her husband Jamie worked as a translation assistant at an ad agency in Toronto. They lived in a small rented house and had three girls, nine, six and four-and-a-half year old. Their annual household income was in the region of $55,000 net of taxes.

When I met Joyce and Jamie at a workshop I was conducting for families from a low-income neighbourhood, they seemed very interested to know more about my methods of achieving financial independence. After the workshop, they approached me and requested for a private meeting. A week later, I met this wonderful couple at my office and spent two hours talking to them.

Five minutes before the appointment time, I looked out the window to see Jamie carefully park his 2012 Honda Civic in the only accessible parking spot outside. As they entered my office, I looked at their confident but seemingly unexcited smiles. I recalled their humble optimism from my brief conversation with them at the workshop. It looked like they were unsure of something. From Joyce's body language I could sense that she was more determined to find out ways to get out of their financial predicament than Jamie; perhaps she had pushed Jamie to come for the appointment that day.

Jamie wore an unremarkable beige jacket over a checkered blue shirt and cotton slacks while Jamie was wearing a pair of blue jeans and a white shirt that had been battered almost out of shape by washing. They looked like the typical working class family with no clue how to find a way out of their negative net worth, and perhaps too ashamed to share their financial situation with others.

As we started talking, Joyce spoke of their family life and the challenges it entailed; she spoke of how much their girls mean to them and how they wanted to create a secure financial future for them. Jamie was mostly quiet but pitched in at constant intervals to complain how much he hated his job. As Jamie and Joyce opened up to me, they felt more comfortable sharing with me what they thought was the worst financial situation a couple in their mid-thirties could be in. They hesitantly showed me some numbers and when I told them that it is a common financial scenario, they looked surprised and relieved at the same time.

Jamie admitted that they had been depending too much on their overdraft facility for the past many months as their household income had been falling short of their monthly expenditure, and that they had zero dollars in emergency funds. Jamie was afraid of finding him in a situation where he would have to look to their friends and family to borrow money because their credit card limits were already busted. Joyce shook her head and added that it would be beyond embarrassing.

I spent almost two hours with Joyce and Jamie that day and by the time they left, we had worked out a step-by-step plan together to reduce dependence on their earned income in the next three years. I could see their doubts give way to a gleeful hope by the time we said goodbye.

I met them again a few months ago; more than two years after that initial meeting. They had achieved much of what appeared impossible when they had first met me, and they were well on their way to achieving financial independence. Joyce and Jamie were still working in their respective professions but they had saved enough that they were able to pay 20% down on a 25-year mortgage. They had their own house and $15,000 invested in mutual funds. They no longer had to pay half their salaries in rent and had rented out the basement of their new house to a small family for $800 a month.

To generate extra income, Jamie was working as a freelance translator for publishing houses in addition to his day job with the ad agency. He had set up a small home office so that he didn't need to leave the house while working on his freelance projects. He had introduced Joyce to some of his clients and she was now able to utilize her graphics design diploma by designing book covers and illustrations for authors and publishers. They both had additional sources of income which helped them invest their savings into income generating assets while at the same time, the value of their house appreciated every year. They had paid off their credit card debts and never turned to credit for big ticket items. They still used their credit cards for smaller purchases but only to benefit from the kickbacks while they made sure they paid off their credit card charges every month.

So how did Joyce and Jamie achieve this? They had simply recognized the monetary value of the extra time they had and converted that time into an additional source of earned income. They were probably half-way through the process of achieving complete financial independence and could already see that they had a lot more money available to spend on their family and on what really mattered (like good education for kids and vacations). Once their passive and portfolio incomes grow to an extent that they wouldn't need to rely on earned income, they would get early retirements and spend their time doing whatever they would like to do—whether or not that earned them extra money.

* * *

So let's take a look at how all of us have an extra source of income called time that mostly remains unutilized. In order to generate earned income, you need your human capital (your health, skills, education—all the factors described above) as well as your time. If you have strong human capital but do not have time to put it to use, you will not be able to generate earned income. Similarly, if you have time but do not have human capital, your time will not convert into earned income. The only way your employer is able to use your human capital to generate income for the organization is by signing a contract that basically says they own your time from 9:00 to 5:00. This way they end up controlling your biggest resource—your time.

By controlling your time, they control your ability to earn money. Your employer places a price tag on your human capital and your time. You have no negotiating power to change that so what you earn (your monthly salary) is hardly enough to make ends meet; or sometimes not enough to even do that.

When you are in such a dire situation, your gut reaction is to work even harder. You work longer hours. You overwork your human capital to a point that your health starts to deteriorate. What you fail to realize is that you have another option. Joyce and Jamie had taken that other option to generate extra income so that they were in a positive cash flow situation and had enough leftover income each month to start investing in passive and portfolio income sources.

The key is to find additional sources of earned income that have the potential to provide you higher rates of earning (dollar per unit time) than your current salary rate. If you are earning $25 per hour working for your employer and you start a gig on the side that is unlikely to fetch you anything more than $25 per hour, it is like working overtime; maybe worse. Jamie was able to get a higher rate working as a freelance translator than as an employee. He was still not happy with the number of clients he had but thanks to Joyce's skill set, he was working towards expanding his client base by creating service bundles that would provide discounted translation and graphics design services as a package.

Secondly, it is important to put aspects of your human capital to work that might be underutilized at present. For example, if you think that your current job as an accountant relies too much on your hard skills (your technical knowledge of accounting) and not so much on your soft skills (e.g. your people skills), you might want to do something on the weekends that makes better use of your underutilized people skills.

It is a good idea to create synergies between your core skill currently utilized by your employer and your underutilized skill. For instance, you can start teaching accounting to college students in the evenings and hence put your accounting knowledge and your people skill to good use by complementing each other. This would generate an additional earned income that is detached from your primary source of earned income. In time, this would help you in one of two ways; it will either surpass your primary earned income so that you can transition into self-employment or help you accumulate enough money to start investing in passive and portfolio income sources. Jamie was able to put his communication and negotiation skills to use by dealing directly with clients while using the same technical skill he continued using at his day job.

I have seen many people transition from being fully dependent on their primary earned income to not needing to work at all. The first step is always to diversify sources of income by creating a secondary source of earned income that is detached from your primary source and at the same time complementary to it.

Remember, you are not just expanding your income but creating capital to diversify into other types of income. If you start relying on two sources of earned income instead of one, and do not use your extra income to invest in assets that would generate passive and portfolio incomes, you haven't achieved much in terms of financial independence.

THE OPPORTUNITY COST OF TIME

A lot of people say to me, "Majid, we don't have that extra time you keep talking about. How do we earn the extra income?" In almost 100% of these cases, once I ask them to break down their average day into hours, they invariably get mind boggled by how much time they waste every single day. What they don't realize is the opportunity cost of time.

We all have the same 24 hours in a day. The way you spend those hours is what makes all the difference. For example, I do not have cable television at home, or any kind of television for that matter. I do like to watch a nice movie once in a while, but I'm not addicted to television. When using the Internet, I am every selective in what I spend my time on. I read up on things that would help me build wealth in my 'personal' and 'financial' balance sheets—the former being my wealth of knowledge and the latter, my financial wealth.

Likewise, we all have infinite choices on how to spend our 24 hours. If you are mindful of the financial value of your time, you would spend your time only on activities that would help you grow personally and help your wealth grow, at present or in the future. It is important to have a strategic plan and to break it down into concrete goals that would determine the activities you need to do in order to achieve those goals. Once you have your goals in sight with a definite deadline, you have to find the best way to utilize your 24 hours to move closer to your goals each day. Once you get on with it, you wouldn't find time for futile activities.

The key is to be aware of the opportunity cost of your time. Every time you set out to do something, ask yourself the question, "Is that the best use of my time at present?" If you think you are missing out on an opportunity by spending your time on a certain activity, you need to reevaluate the cost of doing that activity in terms of the value of the missed opportunity. Once you build a habit of asking yourself this question in your subconscious mind, you'll find all the time in the world to engage in activities that would help generate extra earned income. Carpe diem!

Again, I am often approached by seemingly ambitious individuals looking for ways to progress in their careers and lives. Their most common complaint is not having enough time to do anything beyond what they do between 9:00 to 5:00. When we get into a conversation about interests and leisure, I am baffled at how much time they waste every day in activities that would neither help them progress financially not develop personally. What they waste their time on also doesn't help anyone around them in any meaningful way. I have met people who spend hours every week watching humorous videos on the

Internet and the remaining hours dreaming about a perfect future.

Given the number of distractions we all have in this day and age, a practical way to manage time is simply to write down the activities we commonly engage in during an average week and to evaluate each one of them in terms of its value in our lives. Everyone's assessment of value might be different, but for me an activity that doesn't add value in terms of my personal growth, my financial growth or my family life is not a high priority. You only have to strike out such activities from your list and make sure you allocate your time to the ones that remain in the list.

In terms of planning for the long-term, another effective tool that helps you prioritize your time is to create a future résumé. I created my three-year résumé based on my highest aspirations in life. It is a very personal document that I do not share with anyone and it tells me exactly where I plan to be in the next three years. I usually format it in red fonts and as I accomplish each bullet point, I change the colour to black. What that helps me achieve is prioritization of my time by breaking down each bullet point into actionable goals. Each of my goals then determines what I need to do each day to move towards that goal.

As an example, if a bullet point in your future résumé says that you would want to be a columnist for the New York Times, one of your goals might be building relationships with editors at that publication. Now that goal would determine your daily or weekly activities in order to achieve it, which could include connecting with the editors through social media or meeting them personally at events. The bottom-line is that you have to take a top-down approach to time. You cannot just spend your hours as they come and then wonder why you don't have time to make a meaningful change in life and to do things that matter to you and to those around you.

PART 4

What Lies Beyond

"He who is not contented with what he has, would not be contented with what he would like to have."

—Socrates

Chapter 15

Happiness is Overrated: Learn to be Content

What is happiness? There is no easy answer to that question. Philosophers have argued for centuries as to what the crux of happiness is, exploring the alchemy of human happiness in their own distinct ways. Is it something that exists in the psychological dimension or does it live in the spiritual realm; or is it a social phenomenon?

If the inquiry is linguistic, the meaning of happiness would be "a pleasant emotional state." If it were to take a socio-economic connotation, happiness would mean "a state of general wellbeing." Therefore, the answer to the question will depend on what approach you take—biological, psychological, religious, economic, or philosophical.

However, the way I look at it, one condition is common to all definitions of happiness and that is the existence of the cause of happiness. We are happy because of something; a condition that exists on the outside that elicits the reaction of happiness on the inside. It is an effect that results from a cause and not a cause in itself. As Epictetus said, "Show me one who is sick and yet happy, in peril and yet happy, dying and yet happy, in exile and happy, in disgrace and happy."

Therefore, since happiness comes about as a reaction to a pleasant event, it is bound to be temporary. You wouldn't say, "I'm so happy today because it was my birthday seven weeks ago." For as long as the effect of the event lasts, the feeling lasts. Even in case of an enduring pleasant condition, such as being financially successful, the happiness ebbs away with time. It is like the law of diminishing returns. Although you might feel a sense of gratitude for your economic prosperity every day, your happiness will last only as long as you remain economically prosperous.

Don't get me wrong. I'm not against happiness. In fact, many things I do in an average day make me happy. I consider myself a happy person. However, it is the 'pursuit' of happiness that seems like a delusional concept to me. Events induce emotions; good events induce positive ones, and bad events induce negative ones. It's that simple—and that complicated.

These events are a result of actions; natural as well as human. I'm sure you would agree that other than your own actions, you don't have complete control over the other kinds of actions—that of nature and other humans. Your happiness depends to a large extent on your environment, and when you say you are in pursuit of happiness (and nothing else), what you essentially mean is that you are expecting your environment to act in ways that would elicit an emotion of happiness in your heart. It is exactly as absurd as it sounds.

Ironically, with time you forget that your happiness also depends to some extent on your own actions. You get emotionally vested in your expectations of your environment and its control of your own emotions. If your friends and family act in ways consistent with your expectations, that makes you happy; if they don't, you feel dejected. And even if their actions and reactions make you happy, that feeling dissipates as soon as you are endued with another emotion caused by another event or action not completely in your control. Pursuit of happiness is like chasing a moving target—a target stuck to the belly of a frolicsome kangaroo.

Why would you like to relinquish the control of your emotions to others? If you think that's just the way things are, you need to think again. It is not that pursuit of happiness is the greatest personal virtue; in fact, it is far from being a virtue at all. The greatest virtue is to lead a meaningful life; to have a purposeful existence. If it so happens that you encounter happiness along the way, you are lucky.

So it is not the pursuit of a selfish temporary emotion dependent on uncontrollable factors that is the greatest virtue of them all. Happiness is overrated. It is like sugar, or caffeine. You like eating fancy confectionaries or drinking coffee because you feel the urge to consume something your mind has learned to associate with satisfaction. As soon as the effect of the substance subsides, your urge becomes stronger and you start looking for the next source of the substance you are addicted to. The only party that gains from the seesaw of your appetite is the folks who run the café.

Likewise, we get attracted to flashy gadgets and expensive watches because our minds have learned that buying them yields happiness. Again, by doing that we have relinquished the control of a precious feeling to those who manufacture, price and distribute products. What choice do we have, you must be thinking.

The choice is to create a meaningful life and do the things that fulfil our purpose. Doing those things may or may not lead to happiness, but it is in doing them that we find contentment. Pursuit of contentment therefore should be our goal.

BEING CONTENT

Contentment is not a result of an external event. You are not content because you are rich; you are content despite being poor. Diogenes who Plato called "a Socrates gone mad," once said, "People have the most, when they are most content with the least."

Since contentment does not stem from the environment and is not dependent on it to persist, it endures regardless of the social, economic, emotional or physical state of a person.

When Epictetus said, "Show me one who is sick and yet happy, in peril and yet happy, dying and yet happy, in exile and happy, in disgrace and happy," he was referring to a content soul whose measure of virtue is not material wellbeing, but a spiritual condition of inner peace and solace.

Pursuit of contentment is a virtue because contentment disregards occurrence of an event or a human action as conditions for its origination. Pursuit of contentment is not the pursuit of an elusive tomorrow; it is the celebration of today. In that, it is the pursuit to end all pursuits. Contentment unshackles us from the disquiet of tomorrow and helps us let go of our anxieties and our emotional baggage. It teaches us gratitude, forbearance and forgiveness—qualities necessary to lead a meaningful life.

It makes you rise above the world and transcend the feeling of misery that focusing on your and others' inadequacies creates. Your emotional and spiritual state becomes insulated from the whims of the world around you, and you are free to find the true meaning of life, unhindered by other's interpretation of meaningfulness. Contentment gives you the assurance that you are at ease with yourself right at this moment, just the way you are, and that there is nothing in the world that you need to pursue for your own self.

CONTENTMENT IS NOT COMPLECENCE

A content person is not snug as a bug in a rug. When it comes to human endeavour and attaining meaningfulness in life, he feels a sense of responsibility. This sense of responsibility leads him to live within his means, donate excess belongings, balance work and relationships, and focus on achieving personal excellence. Contentment is a prerequisite for achievement of Maslow's self-actualization. And this is how contentment is a virtue.

Owing to his strong sense of responsibility, the ambition of a content person is not to accumulate wealth for the sake of it, but to use it to make a difference in people's lives, and to use his potential to enhance the potential of others; to solve problems. A content person puts his heart and mind to achieving these goals, but he is not disappointed at the results. He persists in the wake of failures, and carries on his mission because that's what gives meaning to his life, not the results of his efforts. He is satisfied with himself but not with the status quo. He continues to strive whether or not he finds himself in an ideal state of affairs to make a difference. He blooms where he is planted. He is anything but complacent.

That is the defining characteristic of the first dancer. To achieve real success in life, his pursuit of material wealth has a meaning beyond physical wellbeing. He does not rebuff the idea of acquiring wealth but his endeavour for wealth is not his ultimate goal. People whose pursuit of material wealth is founded in contentment rather than in gluttony strive for greatness and not just success. These people leave their legacy behind, not in the form of their possessions but their bestowals to the world; their literature, their inventions, their works of art, their acts of compassion, their labour and their charity.

* * *

To become the first dancer, you have to learn to be content with today, yet pursue a better tomorrow; you have to be content with yourself and yet strive to become better. This is achieved through constant reflection and meditation. You have to learn to be kind to yourself before you could be kind to others. You have to forgive yourself for your inadequacies at present to be at peace with yourself, only to find the courage to address the same inadequacies. It is like being comfortable with being uncomfortable.

The first dancer has the courage to question himself and challenge his thoughts and actions without being anxious or insecure about it. His progression towards betterment is in pursuit of excellence and not success; it is to make him the best version of himself and not merely acceptable to the world. This gives rise to an attitude I call 'arrogant humility.'

The first dancer's arrogant humility is the manifestation of his internal state of equilibrium between his past, present and future. He has no remorse, mortification or guilt for this past. He is confident of and grateful to all that he has at present. And he is hopeful of the future, beyond his selfish desires for the self.

With that state of equilibrium, the first dancer comes across as a pleasant person, confident and self-assured, yet accepting and humble. This attitude is evident in every nuance of his behaviour towards people; in his voice, his body language, his words and his inaction. This is the essence of charismatic leadership that is not inborn but a result of conscientious reflection. The first dancer is Diogenes' ideal human who has the most when he is most content with the least, yet he considers pursuit of excellence his responsibility.

Chapter 16

Wellbeing and the Nature of Work

The Oxford Dictionary defines wellbeing as "the state of being comfortable, healthy, or happy." I believe that the primary endeavour of the human race is the pursuit of this very goal—individual and collective wellbeing at mental, physical and spiritual levels. On the other hand, we have been bogged down in a never-ending discussion on work-life balance for many decades as if work is necessarily antithetical to wellbeing.

Work itself—whether looked at as an inescapable exigency to provide sustenance or as a vocation to reach one's highest potential—is not to be blamed for the universal predicament that most of humanity finds itself in today. Most people consider making a living a burden to bear not because they have to work towards it but because the work they have to do is unavailing of the conditions required to create wellbeing. Ironically, the demands of building a career in today's world steer us away from achieving wellbeing—the very purpose we deem a career is meant to fulfil. As I implied in the MBA's last resignation letter in chapter 13, we have successfully fooled ourselves into believing that building a career is akin to building a life.

THE NATURE OF WORK

A report titled, "Mental Capital and Wellbeing: Making the most of ourselves in the 21st century"[1] published as part of the UK Government's Foresight Project to advise the Government and the private sector on how to achieve the best possible mental development and mental wellbeing, noted, "While all advanced economies have experienced a shift from manufacturing towards services... it is continuing almost unabated. Whether this change is best characterised as a post-industrial society, a knowledge-based economy, a network economy or a new economy, what is clear, is that the 'economy is becoming increasingly weightless'[2]. The 'weightless' idea, as Coyle and Quah[3] describe, is where 'creating value depends less and less on physical mass, and more and more on intangibles, such as human intelligence, creativity, and even personal warmth'".

This has been the singular most significant characteristic of the paradigm shift in economic models over the past centuries. In both service- and product-based models, we

---

[1] Dewe, P. and Kompier, M. (2008) Foresight Mental Capital and Wellbeing Project. Wellbeing and work: Future challenges. The Government Office for Science, London
[2] Coyle and Quah (2002) p.8
[3] Ibid

have moved farther and farther away from the use of tangible and natural factors of production to complex multi-faceted means of value creation. While on the one hand, this has clearly benefitted the world economy at a macro level by creating more efficient business and production models, enabling collaboration and cross-pollination of innovative ideas, and spreading the effects of economic propensity to masses far and wide, on the other hand it has made the concept of holistic wellbeing an elusive dream.

This discussion is interlaced with the discussion we had on the opportunity cost of time in chapter 14. An important factor responsible for the deterioration of our overall wellbeing has been poor prioritization of time, which is largely devoid of any semblance of human purpose. We work either because we consider it necessary to survive, or because we desire to get the economic means to go beyond mere survival into building a good life in terms of material prosperity. In other words, work is related to either survival and sustenance or to material wellbeing.

Holistic wellbeing is either considered a fantastic notion that only exists in fairytales, or is something we have grown totally unaware of. Still, at the foundation of holistic wellbeing is an equilibrium between our heart's desire to find our labour of love—our overarching human purpose on the one hand, and our need for physical and mental wellbeing on the other. While the societal and economic models prevalent in the world today dictate a nature of work that is designed to promote attainment of the latter, it is unfortunately at the cost of the former; and hence the concept of holistic wellbeing remains an unachievable goal.

Moreover, due to the popularization of the role of intermediaries in the modern economic models and the resultant complexity of value creation chains, work has moved farther away from the natural factors of production, primarily land. We are seldom involved in a process that produces the food we eat. This in turn has led to rapid urbanization and the associated lifestyle changes. These lifestyle changes have led us away from physical and mental wellbeing by raising stress to unprecedented levels. It has also imposed unreasonable demands on us from time management perspective.

Collectively, all of the above has adversely affected our ability to attain holistic wellbeing and if we track the causes of this effect back to the original cause, we will find that the historic evolution of economic models—most prominently, the industrial revolution and the twentieth century trade liberalization—has been at the helm of the eventual retrogression of human wellbeing.

YOU ARE BIGGER THAN YOUR CAREER

The Soviet novelist, Chingiz Aitmatov recounted a story in one of his articles written near the end of the failed Marxist movement in Soviet Union.

In 1935, Stalin invited his trusted senior advisors and some media henchmen to a meeting with intent to make a point using the most evocative of methods. When everyone was gathered at the barnyard, he called for a live chicken and vigorously clenched it in one hand. With the other hand, he then began to pluck out the chicken's feathers in handfuls. The poor bird squawked under the torment but Stalin kept at denuding the chicken until it convulsed with agony. Remarkably unperturbed by the feeling of disgust obvious on the faces of the people too afraid to express their unease to the dictator, he continued until the chicken was completely unfeathered.

He then put the bird down by a small heap of grain and stood up to finish the last act while the people curiously observed the chicken move towards the grain. As the chicken started to peck, Stalin put his hand into his jacket pocket and pulled out another fistful of grain, putting it out in front of the wounded bird. To the utter surprise of the transfixed spectators, the chicken managed a wick-kneed stagger back to Stalin and started to peck the fresh grain right out of the hand that moments ago had inflicted unbearable pain on it. Stalin had made his point—loud and clear.

He turned to the people and said, "People are like this chicken. It doesn't matter how much pain you inflict on them. The moment you offer them what they need, they will still follow you and turn to you for their survival."

To me this anecdote has another, slightly different meaning. It is not 'despite' the pain that Stalin inflicted on the poor bird, but 'because of it' that it followed him. This explains the working of weak minds—animals' as well as humans'. Our minds become slaves to those we see as having total power to control us and to cause pain to us. We are quick to give up control of ourselves to those who have the power to rule us as long as they also have the power to feed us. This is the fundamental construct of a feudal society.

The series of events that transpired since the industrial revolution determined the dynamics of today's social and economic hierarchies. The world saw a polarizing division between the powerful and the weak. It got divided into those who controlled the factors of production and those who worked for the former and depended on them for survival; the employer and the employee—the haves and the have-nots if you will.

The private control of capital coupled with a liberal new structure for the free-market made the poor rich and the rich richer. Private enterprises boomed and commercial ownership got decentralized, but something else happened as well. Amid the much-ballyhooed advent of private business ownership and birth of the 'corporation,' a parallel layer in the economic hierarchy was created—those who controlled the owners of private businesses. Paradoxically, it was the centralization of decentralization, the former being invisible to the masses. This was the new face of feudalism.

This made the working class dream a mere fantasy. There was no way you could rise up the ranks to be among the top economic powers by working for the private enterprise. That was simply not part of the deal. Instead, you would be given a certain dollar amount for the time you spent away from your family at the cost of your holistic wellbeing; and with that money, you may buy whatever you wish to buy—goods produced by the same private enterprise—in order to survive and stay healthy enough to turn up for work the next morning. But you dare not demand anything more. Capitalism was born.

With that, we all became salary slaves—too afraid to raise our voices against our providers and oppressors, lest we be laid off. We had willingly given up our freedom in exchange of economic security. Our inner calling and our human purpose took the back seat because for us a more pressing issue was to put food on the table for our children. We did not control the land, nor the industry built atop the land, nor the labour who worked there. We were that labour, and we did not control ourselves. We did not control our time, or our actions. The dream of finding our inner calling was lost forever. And we were so busy surviving that we forgot to live.

People started defining their self-worth by the name of the corporation they worked for. The more reputable the brand name, the more accomplished they felt. And then they were nothing more than what they did between 9:00 to 5:00 in order to survive; it became their identity as their real human identity got lost somewhere in the smoke of the chimneys from all the factories. This breed of employees comprised of millions of educated and uneducated individuals, men and women, who were so ignorant of the potential of their minds and spirits that they had proudly set the bar low for themselves.

The truth is, we are like Stalin's chicken, pecking the grains out of our tormentor's hand in order to barely survive. We call this our 'career' and adorn our chests with it like shiny badges of chivalry. It is a great complement to call someone career-oriented, not worrying too much about what the tradeoff involves. The truth is that the very definition of modern career is an exchange of one's freedom for sustenance.

For the first dancer, the measure of a successful life is more than a career. He is bigger than his career, and his true self is unshackled not when he has figured out how to best meet his physiological needs, but when he doesn't have to worry about his physiological needs anymore. He can put the incredible faculty of his mind to more productive and meaningful uses than to make a living. It surely helps to be economically independent, but the first dancer does not need to be outrageously opulent to make the transition into a career-free life, he merely needs to be reasonably self-sufficient and content with his material wellbeing.

An additional complexity may arise even after you have insulated your financial position from the ups and downs of your career. That complexity is over-reliance on your knowledge and skills to earn your income. Recall how earned income is essentially based on the work you do—your active employment of your skills, education and talent. This unfortunately is dependent on the demand for your skillset which may change with time, thereby affecting your ability to generate earned income.

As I will explain in chapter 18, there is a good rationale of diversifying your sources of income (whether earned, passive or portfolio) into primary sources of value. That would include natural resources like land, energy sources and minerals. The kind of financial independence that arises from such diversification is far more sustainable over the long run and helps you concentrate on achieving your true human potential without needing to worry about building a career.

Chapter 17

Don't Let Success Come in the Way of Your Excellence

You can find millions of books and articles on success, but hardly any on excellence. In order to emulate the people who achieved excellence, the readers use instant tutorials guaranteeing success. What they don't know is that the success of the people they seek to follow was a byproduct of their pursuit of excellence.

I realized mid-career that pursuit of success could be a trap. It may lead you astray from the path of excellence—the quintessential exemplification of human endeavour. Success is like an instant boost of energy we need to get through the present moment. It nourishes our ego and mends our low self-esteem. It makes us look good to the world. But once we are through with the present moment and the effect of the energy booster subsides, we realize that it sapped us of the strength we needed to excel in life.

For most people, there is a tradeoff between success and excellence—a compromise they settle for because they are too afraid to *not* succeed. Striving for excellence means letting go of your immediate opportunities for success. It means having the grit and patience to consciously choose delayed gratification. It means changing course every time you find yourself close to your destination, and it necessitates casting out your sense of entitlement and your pride. Excellence happens when there is no room for complacence that success conspires to create in your heart.

The fact that so many people stop just short of achieving excellence in their careers points to the flaws in our educational and economic systems. I have no doubt in my mind that excellence is inevitable if your vocation is your passion. If what you do is in complete sync with your inner calling and your sense of purpose in life, you are bound to excel in it. However unfortunately, so few of us find our inner calling in life.

As young children, we are taught that the measure of excellence is how successful we are compared to those around us. Students are more eager to pass the test than to learn the lesson and make that learning part of their character. They grow negligent to their talents and their purpose. As a result, an entire generation of workers is born instead of a generation of thinkers and achievers.

Our education prepares us to make a living doing something which has good potential of earning us money in the foreseeable future. It is completely devoid of any semblance of discovery of our talents and passions. We do end up in vocations that pay us reasonably well and we are able to make ends meet too, but that's where our success starts to hinder our excellence. An overwhelming majority of people I interviewed over the past couple of years admitted that they are not satisfied with the jobs they have been at since several years. I suspect the rest of the people did not feel comfortable enough to admit that.

Success and excellence do not necessarily have to be mutually exclusive. Whereas many of us give up the pursuit of excellence because we are too complacent with our success and to us giving up our success to start anew in the path of excellence is akin to accepting failure, the truth is that our successes could be our stepping stones to excellence. I used to think that success is the path to excellence. The truth is, successes are like milestones while excellence is a never-ending journey. You may meet many successes on your path of excellence, but your successes must not deviate you from this path.

If you started a dozen companies that failed before you achieved success as an entrepreneur, you did not settle for anything less than excellence because you knew what your inner calling was. What you also had was an awareness that the path of failure you chose for yourself led you closer to your vision of entrepreneurial excellence. That is the laser-sharp focus that excellence is made of.

THE ART OF EXCELLENCE

First, it is crucial to understand what the prerequisites for excellence are. Pursuit of excellence presupposes an awareness of your inner calling and a strategic vision of your future.

A person who has these two will not think twice before giving up everything in pursuit of excellence. Such people have no regrets for having pivoted back to their trajectory of excellence because they were aware of their inner calling. They have a sense of purpose and deep in their hearts they feel that they have been bestowed with the talents needed to achieve that purpose.

In order to achieve excellence you have to have a certain method in your madness. First, you have to dream so big that it would scare you. It should shake up your self-regard and force you to take yourself seriously. But then you have to be open to try out different ways of exploring what you have been given. Most people don't know what their talents are for and what the nature's plan for them is. Discovering your inner calling or the vocation you were meant to pursue takes trial and error. This requires courage and patience and this is precisely where you have to decide; success now or excellence later. Soon, there will be no time for trial and error and your commitment to excellence will demand your undivided focus. It is critical to understand that this is an unconventional path with many challenges greeting you at every step. The path of trial and error has dire economic implications and a social stigma attached to it.

Secondly, people who excel in their lives have a vision of where they want to be. Once they have figured out what they have a real passion for and what wakes them up every morning, they are no longer dreamers. They turn into doers. They become strategic thinkers and meticulous planners.

Remember, there are no shortcuts to excellence. Excellence is a lot of hard work; and it's not all labour of love. The drudgery of putting your head down and doing whatever it takes to excel is what distracts most people from the pursuit of excellence, especially when the alternatives look so glamourous in contrast. As a result, they settle for success—the instant gratification they derive from praise, fanfare and accolades.

Hence the most important lesson is to realize that working for excellence is not a bed of roses. You must know that there is a reason why most people do not pursue this path. They either 'decide' to settle for mediocrity at a young age or they simply remain ignorant most of their lives and by the time they recognize their inner calling, they figure it is too late to set out on the path to excellence.

As a mentor, my heart aches for all the gifted people I meet and speak with so often. Their immense potential gleams in their eyes yet they are unaware of their own talents. They seem to have willingly set the bar low for themselves only because years ago they were made to accept a certain definition of success by people who had no right to define what success meant for them. They do not know what lies beyond their next promotion, their next salary raise, their next best employee award. Success; not excellence; is an unending pursuit for them. They have a nice car but they want a better one; they have a comfortable house, but they want a bigger one. They are heedless that their daily dose of caffeinated success suppresses their appetite for excellence. And just when the effect of caffeine wears out, they want another dose, leading them astray from the path of excellence again.

Then there are those who think they're after excellence, when in fact they misconceive excellence as doing the same thing over and over again like an endless loop, and being satisfied with that. To them, this is contentment.

I met Jorge Padilla after a talk I delivered to a group of young accounting professionals in Hamilton, Ontario. He seemed like an average white-collar guy satisfied with his life and work. At first I did not even notice him in the small audience of around 20 people. After the talk, he walked over to me and we started to have a chat. I learned that Jorge worked at a company in Toronto and commuted over 60 kilometers to be at work every morning at 9:00. In his late 30's and visibly fatigued, Jorge had been at the same job for the last 17 years. My jaw almost dropped when I heard that he had been promoted just once during that time, from Junior Tax Analyst to Tax Analyst. I never got a chance to meet Jorge again, but a year later I met another gentleman who reminded me of Jorge.

This time, the person was a highly qualified procurement engineer at a large industrial plant in Alberta. I met Elson at a networking event I was invited to by a friend. The handout mentioned that the program would include a couple of presentations by prominent visual artists, an optional photography workshop and an art exhibition. Being more interested in the exhibition than in the workshop, I decided to skip the latter and stood by a large metallic sculpture trying to make sense of what looked like a pointless concoction of scrapped bottle caps and twister pieces of steel.

Along came Elson, a well-dressed middle-aged man wearing a serious look on his bearded face. I was too engrossed in the sculpture to notice a person standing right by my side, until I heard a polite 'hi.' He had apparently stepped out of the photography workshop that had started only five minutes back. We started talking. We had spoken for only a couple of minutes when I realized that I was perhaps in the company of a master artist. His passion about art further affirmed my presumption. Well, I was totally wrong.

Elson introduced himself as a mechanical engineer working for a manufacturing company. He must have noticed my bewilderment because he immediately chuckled, "I'm also a photographer on the side." I asked him why he had decided to ditch the workshop and he said that it was too basic for his use. We spoke for the next half hour during which I realized he was the complete opposite of the snobs I knew at that time in the artist community. Elson was not just well-versed in arts, he had an assertive personality and was very down to earth—a combination you don't see every day. Finding that he was in downtown Toronto for the week, I invited him over for coffee the next day. What I discovered about Elson got me completely dumbfounded.

He showed me some of the photographs he had taken over the years and I was spellbound for a moment. He did not have a website, or a Facebook page or anything else to showcase his phenomenal photographic talent to the world. Having been responsible for marketing of products for many years, I had seen numerous pitches involving photographs and artworks from some very talented artists. Sometimes, I was fascinated by their brilliant works of art; at other times, I had mumbled to myself, "It would be better if this person had chosen a different vocation." Yet, here was this average looking guy who had been working as an engineer at the same company for 11 years, showing me a portfolio I could assuredly rate higher than some of the best I had ever seen.

My obvious next question to Elson was, "Why are you an engineer Elson?" He disclosed that he came from a long line of engineers and how becoming an engineer was a no-brainer, not only because that was the in thing in his family but also because he thought that was what he aspired to do in life. As I raised an eyebrow, he quickly added "I realized later, I wasn't born to be an engineer. I was meant to be an artist." "A recessive gene perhaps," I added and we both laughed.

Elson was a textbook case of a professional who had given up his passion for his profession; he had given up excellence for success. I can't begin to imagine where he would have landed as an artist had he spent all these years doing what he had a true passion for instead of buying raw materials for manufacturing kitchen appliances. The fact that he had achieved so much success in his career was a testament to his positive attitude and hard work, but in a profession not aligned with his inner calling, those elements could only get him this far; they could not lead him beyond success. And being one of the most senior people in the department where he had accomplished a lot over the past many years, he cherished the respect he got from his peers. His expertise was virtually unquestionable.

I felt that Elson was beholden to his company and everyone who worked there for giving him that respect. He was a smart cookie and maybe even realized that he was a slave to his success. I am not sure if it was a conscious decision on his part to neglect the promising prospect of him becoming an excellent visual artist, but his eyes glowed with an extraordinary avidity at my mere suggestion of him starting a small business on the side to bring his talents into service for people in my network who could be among his first clients and patrons. Maybe he was just waiting for someone to provide him the reassurance that what he had was indeed valuable.

Elson and his family have since moved to Vancouver where he now runs a very successful company that owns many studios offering photography, filmmaking and animation services to international clients. He is not just successful at what he does, he *feels* he is successful. To me, he discovered his inner calling and excelled at it.

EXCELLENCE AND MONEY

So does it mean that when you follow your passion and do what you love to do, you excel at it and *also* achieve financial success? Incorrect! At least in the short term you don't.

And unfortunately, that is precisely where people get it all wrong. Doing what you love to do may not make you financially successful; in fact there are lesser chances of you making it big money-wise if what you love doing is not the best commercial proposition out there. To me, excellence entails being the best at what you love to do, and also achieving financial success doing it. Therefore, only the former is not enough in order to achieve excellence; you have to convert your passion into an economic success. In fact, as far as your passion is concerned, the hard truth is nobody really cares about it as much as you do.

Let me explain it this way. Had Elson just picked up his camera and gone backpacking to New Zealand (which sure sounds like a lot of fun), he would not have achieved excellence doing what he loved doing. Still, he would have had great time doing it. But then, maybe a few days or weeks later when he had run out of all the money, he might have realized how crazy that idea was. This would have him believe that following your passion and doing what you love doing is not such a good idea after all.

So just assuming that people will be concerned about your passion just because you love the work is like getting carried away with your optimism without giving much thought to how to make it their business first. I see a lot of people ending up into the same pit where they started. They find themselves stuck in a zero sum game, spending the same—or greater—number of hours doing what they were doing before but not making as much as before. Without evidence of short- to medium-term financial success, the dream of economic freedom and the charm of being your own boss dissipate.

So here's the deal. Doing something you aren't meant to do but are financially successful doing makes you regret it in the long run. Doing what you love to do but not achieving financial success doing it makes you regret it even sooner. It is like running after your self-actualization need before having met your physiological need.

Doing what you love doing *and* making it into a financial success is what keeps you on the path to excellence. Therefore, it is imperative to consider your passion as just another business and apply the same business planning principles you would to any other business. Ask yourself the following questions.

- Why are you doing what you are doing and what is your mission?

- What problem are you solving for your clients and what value are you creating for them?
- How are you using your unique value to solve their problem and how are you positioning it?

It follows from the above that in order to achieve excellence you have to employ your skills and talents in many areas at the same time. Elson was successful at his business not only because he was exceptional at the core skill but also because he had the business experience of working with vendors and partners. He had great negotiation and business planning skills. Also, apart from having a remarkable aesthetic sense, he was a qualified engineer—mentally ambidextrous so to speak.

In history, we have so many other examples of people who absolutely loved what they did and truly excelled at it because they put their complementary skills and talents to use. Pablo Picasso and Thomas Alva Edison are among the most prominent.

Chapter 18

The Miracle in Your Head

Who would you give credit to for all that the human race has achieved since millennia? What would you consider the single most important factor in defining the evolution of the human civilization on earth? To me, it is the human mind, and it is nothing short of a miracle.

To understand the power of the human mind (*your* mind), look no further than the advancements that have been made in technology only in the past three to four decades. It is mindboggling how the human mind has harnessed not only the powers of nature but also the power of the human mind itself. This is the defining moment; we are entering a new era—the Singularity.

This is unlike anything human civilization has ever seen before. This is where it gets unfathomable. This is where the lines get blurred; the lines between natural creation and human invention, the lines between microchips and human genome, the lines between artificial intelligence and human consciousness—the lines between non-human and human. The Singularity is an era in which each moment is a revolution. It is the time when the only thing humans will be certain of is the uncertainties that engulf them like a million moths invading a standing crop. The future will be inescapable.

Over the last many centuries, the human mind has been on the driving seat of technological advancements. This is going to change markedly. In Singularity, the human mind will be tested to its core; the challenge would not be to achieve the next level of technological advancements but to keep pace with it. To understand the power of what is about to be unleashed in the years to come will be our biggest challenge. And whether or not this power is good, is unknown at best.

THE SINGULARITY

It is impossible to define the unknown. The very definition of Singularity is that it is the unseen and the unanticipated. Hence, by definition, it is undefinable.

For me, the purpose of writing about this most significant development in human civilization is not to inculcate fear in your mind or to instigate your natural fight or flight syndrome. The purpose is to call your attention to the unprecedented nature of the phenomenon that is not subject to any ifs and buts, and that has already progressed to a point of no return. To excel as humans and maximize the potential of the miracle we have all been bestowed with, you ought to be aware of the era you and your next generation are setting foot in. Within our lifetime, we will see such remarkable advancements in technology that it would necessitate a rethinking of the entire socio-economic structure of the human civilization. This would inevitably have an impact on your human potential and your economic competitiveness.

In a way, everything that will ever happen to each and every human being is the subject matter for a discussion on the 'future of humanity.' This includes what your great-great-granddaughter will have for lunch on a given Saturday many many years from now. It is beyond reasonability to even attempt to predict to that level of granularity what the future might bring in the lives of human beings. However, since the Singularity will have altered the foundations of causality beyond anyone's wildest imaginations, it would in fact determine what your great-great-granddaughter will have for lunch on a given Saturday many many years from now.

So what really is this Singularity? To me, it has three key postulates. Number one, it will alter our perception of reality itself, if not the nature of it, in such a way that it will be unexplainable to people from all previous civilizations. Second, it will be characterized by convergence to a single source of power and intelligence. And lastly, the rate of technological advancement will be exponential. Pretty unbelievable, right? Well, the truth is we are already well underway to create a future that will have all the three characteristics. If you consider this an exaggeration, examine the following.

The theoretical affordance of the concept points to five inevitable conditions that form the basis for the humanity entering the era of Singularity. First, computers improve and get faster. Second, the rate at which computers get faster accelerates. Third, humans create a computer better than the human mind. Fourth, the computer makes another computer smarter than itself. Five, this cycle continues until the humanity enters Singularity.

Now, although all the above five conditions may not be true to the same degree, they are all true nonetheless—some more than others. For example, I wouldn't argue against the first condition. We all know that computers are getting faster. However, when we look at the second condition, it might not fit into the straitjacket of what Moore's Law predicted in terms of the rate of acceleration due to the cyclical fluctuations we have observed in that rate and also due to the fact that the transistor technology would reach a certain plateau, warranting a fundamental rethinking of how computing should happen, much like the transition from vacuum tubes to transistors in the first place. Nevertheless, the condition holds true.

It gets remarkably more interesting when you examine the next three conditions associated with the advent of Singularity. The logical sequence of technological progression from this point on culminates at what I term 'technological infinitum.'

The reason Singularity is unlike any era of human civilization in the past is because it will achieve technological infinitum—the infinite ability of technology to create better technology. When that happens, many of my writer friends will have to look for alternative careers because there will be no genre in literature called science fiction. The distinction between reality and fiction will cease to exist as humanity enters the realm of transhumanism. The word 'possibility' will have a different meaning in Singularity as humans become post-humans.

According to a paper titled, "The Future of Humanity," written by Nick Bostrom[4] of the Future of Humanity Institute at Oxford University, transhumanism refers to "a condition which has at least one of the following characteristics: population greater than one trillion persons, life expectancy greater than 500 years, large fraction of the population has cognitive capacities more than two standard deviations above the current human maximum, near-complete control over the sensory input for the majority of people for most of the time, human psychological suffering becoming rare occurrence, [and] any change of magnitude or profundity comparable to that of one of the above."

The Singularity will usher in an era in which the combined human intelligence will be of transhuman proportions as it gets interweaved with synthetic intelligence (human brain implanted with the self-learning computer

---

[4] Bostrom, N. (2007) "The Future of Humanity," *New Waves in Philosophy of Technology*, Palgrave McMillan, 2009: 186-216

technology of the future). In other words, as paradoxical (and confusing) as it may sound, the human intelligence will have created an intelligence more intelligent than itself and capable of creating an intelligence more intelligent than it, until the possibility reaches infinity.

The way things look right now, there is nothing stopping us from entering Singularity. Look at the scientific research and technological advancements of the present day. Who would have thought that we would be well past the stage of decoding the human genome and actually thinking of ways to alter the human gene to achieve superhuman capabilities and end disease? Parallel to the pure biological stream of research, a major breakthrough has been the interconnectivity of the brain cell with the microchip, giving rise to the possibility of a symbiotic relationship between the human brain and machine. Imagine humans becoming an extension of the Internet of things, with millions of nanobots running in your blood stream, repairing your body seamlessly and boosting its natural defense mechanism against disease. Considering that there is nothing stopping us from achieving a feat like that suddenly makes Bostrom's 500-year old human sound a little less fictional.

Similar advancements in physical human augmentation such as the progressive research and development in the field of robotic exoskeleton have allowed us to anticipate a future where humans would turn into post-humans, capable of accomplishing unimaginable physical performance.

IMPLICATIONS AT PRESENT

The fact that much of our headway to Singularity may happen in the next few decades makes the preceding discussion extremely relevant for us. Ignoring it as hypothetical or fictional at present will have dire consequences for us all in the near future. Traditional occupations as we know them may become obsolete sooner than we anticipated. In the next few decades, the measure of human skill and intelligence will change, thereby impacting the economic potential and the ability of households to generate income.

The concepts presented in the preceding chapters therefore become all the more important in that they underscore the need to diversify your skillset, optimize the use of time and enhance your economic potential at present to create financial independence in the future. It is critical to think beyond the next few years and to preempt what the long-term future might hold for you and your next generations as we enter Singularity.

Recall our discussion on the evolution of economic models that pushed us farther and farther away from the natural sources of economic value creation to more 'artificial' means. Alongside that, the creation of intermediary value chains in the production cycle has given birth to new vocations. On the other hand, many professions have gone obsolete or are at the verge of obsolescence after a surprisingly short lifespan. While the advent of the knowledge economy was a major turning point for human civilization, the way it was unremarkable was that it did not cut off our connection with the natural resources that provide the basis for human sustenance and technological advancement. There is no silicon chip without silicon and there is no electricity without water, wind, sunlight and coal.

So unless the human race harnesses the power to 'create,' I do not foresee nature becoming irrelevant in Singularity. As a corollary of this premise, a reasonable strategy is to try and achieve financial independence not only by diversifying into alternative income sources that increasingly rely on human knowledge, but by controlling natural resources (land, energy sources, minerals etc.). This solidifies my suggestion of building a strong balance sheet in order to achieve sustainable wealth for yourself and your future generations.

Final Word

Moments Create Momentum

When you think about your dream—what you are striving to achieve in life—I am sure you have some plan; some routine you follow day in and day out to get there and to make it happen. Maybe you are moving forward. Maybe you are in a rough spot. But regardless of your situation in life, there are certainly untapped opportunities. And these opportunities, they just sit there waiting to be had. They *will* sit there for an eternity if you don't recognize them and utilize them.

These opportunities are nothing but moments in your life. If you are not willing to ask yourself, "How can I make the best of this moment," you won't grow to the level you are capable of. You are missing the key ingredient to success.

Remember, moments create momentum. That phone call you never made, that email you never sent, or that handshake that would have changed the path for you; they were all opportunities you missed. These moments could open up a sea of opportunities only if you made the best of them right when they were presented to you. Or they may just pass as fragments of time not leaving a trace of regret because you never realized what you missed.

Every moment counts; even the ones you spend watching funny cat videos on YouTube. Well, I have nothing against cats, but imagine if you could take that half hour and reallocate it to sending three emails to people who have been successful in their fields, whether you know them or not; where would it get you? See if you can connect, if you can have a valuable conversation. Maybe it would result in nothing, or maybe it would create a relationship that changes your whole life. Who knows! But I can tell you this for damn sure; the cat video will not do that for you.

I understand that positive thinking is crucial, but merely positive thinking is not enough. Action is crucial, but merely action is not enough. Action *with purpose* is crucial, but merely action with purpose is not enough. It is all these *and* your ability to seize the moments that determines your success in life. Moments is the stuff that opportunities are made of. Why? Because if leveraged consistently, these moments create *momentum*—the consistent reliance on positive action that opens doors for you and knocks down walls. What creates real success is continuous forward hyper momentum. Never undermined the moments.

As we learned in chapter 14, like money, time has an opportunity cost. Unless you make a habit of asking yourself, "Is this the best use of my time at present," you will not realize the opportunity cost of time. You will see a truckload of opportunities pass right in front of your eyes and you wouldn't even realize what you just missed. I guess ignorance is bliss for some!

There have been innumerable experiences in my life when the smallest of gestures created opportunities for me only because I decided to act at the spur of the moment. Whether it was walking over to have a brief chat with the speaker after his keynote address, or sending a thank you email after a brief encounter with someone at a networking event, my moments determined my *possibilities* in the future.

This is the singular most important determinant of what we call luck. A lot of people now come to me and say that I have been lucky. I find it mildly amusing that they only count my successes. If I told them that my successes represent only 1% of the chances I took, I'm sure they would be able to do the math to count my failures. I made the best of the moments I had, but not all of them created opportunities for success. Sometimes I achieved success; other times, I learned. Either way I ended up winning.

Throughout this book, I have shown you examples of people who discovered the real value of the open secret called time. Joyce, Jamie, Santonio and Elson; all made the best of their moments one way or the other. They all had the success mindset, they were creators of their circumstance and not victims of it, they were willing to reinvent themselves, they had attitudinal leadership ingrained in their psyche and they all had bias for action. To me, they were all first dancers. That is how they created opportunities out of thin air.

You too can attract unlimited opportunities like them if you follow what has been presented in this book and take it as a guide to personal development, not as a tutorial for achieving success. Remember, your success is but a means to achieve excellence; your wealth merely a tool to create a legacy for your generations to be proud of.

If this booked touched your heart, I would love to hear from you. If you think it can help someone you know, please feel free to pass it on. Please share what you learned from this book by emailing me at info@thefirstdancer.com. Until we meet again, take care of yourselves.

Acknowledgements

Just like any worthwhile endeavor, writing a book is not possible without the support and encouragement of people around you. I'm afraid I would not be able to express ample gratitude to all those who not only encouraged me to put down my thoughts on paper, but also contributed to my learning experience over the past many years that has become the subject matter of this book.

First and foremost, I thank God for providing me the courage to pursue my dreams despite the many obstacles I faced on the way. I am grateful for His countless blessings.

I owe a great deal to my parents whose unconditional love and kindness showed me the way to a future that would entail unlimited opportunities for learning. They told me that the things that really mattered were not found in the world out there, but inside you. They encouraged me to look inward to achieve real peace and solace; to find the courage and resilience that would get me through the toughest of times, and the sense of gratitude that would challenge my sense of entitlement every time I achieved success. They told me that one's value is determined by what he gives; not what he takes. They told me that the true test of a person's character is how he treats the people around him, and how the society benefits from all that he has to offer; not how much material wealth he accumulates. And this formed the core of my self-belief; the moral compass of my life's work in the years to come. This belief has been the cornerstone of my learning.

I would like to acknowledge the support of my family; my wife who always encouraged me to reach for higher goals and who stood by my side despite all the hardships we faced. Her steadfastness has been a great source of encouragement for me. If she had not shared my burdens, I would not have risen from the falls I had. I owe her my most profound gratitude and my sincerest respect.

My daughter, seven-year old now, knew exactly when to cheer me up throughout the writing of this book. Every time I would hit the writer's block, she would know I needed a little push just by looking at my fingers firmly resting on my forehead with my eyes closed. She would walk up to me and stand by the desk, "daddy, do you need tea?" I would give her a hug and say "No, thank you sweetheart" and a sudden flow of creativity would start gushing down my veins.

I am grateful to my brothers and to their families who believed in me and encouraged me to document my learning over the past many years. I am grateful to Mark McMaster who gave me my first professional break in Canada by asking me for my resume at the end of a five-minute conversation. That opportunity helped me learn a great deal about the Canadian workplace and opened up doors to contribute to a great organization.

I owe my gratitude to Valerie Gow and Allison Pond for connecting me with some extraordinary people in their networks. Thanks to Karen Lior and Alim Maherali for giving me the opportunity to serve on the board of Toronto Workforce Innovation Group—my first board position in Canada. I'm also grateful to the former Consul General of Pakistan in Toronto, Mr. Asghar Ali Golo for his guidance and support as a mentor.

My special thanks to my friend Mazhar Ali Zafar for this guidance, encouragement and support in all my endeavours since the day I moved to Canada. Many of the things I was able to accomplish would not have been possible without his selfless help throughout the years.

My gratitude to all those who agreed to review the manuscript and provide their invaluable feedback and comments, in particular Kevin Kruse, New York Times bestselling author, Senator Hon. Salma Ataullahjan, Member of the Senate of Canada, and Faisal Kutty, professor of law, columnist and public speaker.

Finally, thanks to Chris Dowswell for the photograph and to Maduranga Nuwan for the lovely cover design.

About the Author

Majid Kazmi is a social entrepreneur, investor, and board member based in Toronto, Canada. He is the co-founder and CEO of *Valu Ventures Inc. (www.valuventures.ca)*, a unique social enterprise that supports startup businesses run by immigrant entrepreneurs.

Born and raised in Karachi Pakistan, Kazmi is regarded as a self-made success story. He started his career at J.P. Morgan and has been a career banker for the past one and a half decade. He serves on the boards of *Toronto Workforce Innovation Group* and *H2O4ALL*. He is also advisor to many organizations and think tanks in Canada.

Over the past many years, he has delivered hundreds of talks to audiences big and small, from top universities to billion-dollar blue-chip corporations. He writes for *The Huffington*

Post and many other publications. His articles cover a wide range of topics from business and innovation to personal growth and career success.

As an immigrant success story, Kazmi has been featured on many media outlets in Canada and outside, including Canadian Broadcasting Corporation (CBC) television and radio. In Canada, he is regarded as a leading authority on diversity and inclusion, and immigrant entrepreneurship. Majid holds an MBA from IBA Karachi and is a member of the Harvard Business Review Advisory Council.

How to contact the author

- Visit his personal website: www.majidkazmi.com
- Follow him on Twitter: @majidkazmi1
- View his LinkedIn profile: www.linkedin.com/in/majidkazmi
- Or simply send an email to contact@majidkazmi.com

 the First Dancer

Congratulations!

You took the first big step to become the First Dancer: reading this book. Bravo!

In order to continue learning the secrets of becoming the first among equals and attracting unlimited opportunities, you have to make the most of all the other resources we have created for you.

FREE Resources

- Subscribe to our mailing list on *www.thefirstdancer.com*
- Visit our Facebook page, *www.facebook.com/thefirstdancer*
- Follow us on Twitter, @thefirstdancer
- Join the LinkedIn group, The First Dancer

WIN Big!

We would be delighted to hear your feedback to further improve the next editions of The First Dancer.

Provide your reviews on Amazon.com and send the link to info@thefirstdancer.com to be eligible to receive a signed hardcover copy of Majid Kazmi's next book **absolutely FREE** along with a surprise gift worth **$100**.

For feedback or queries, visit **www.thefirstdancer.com** or write an email to **info@thefirstdancer.com**.

www.ingramcontent.com/pod-product-compliance
Lightning Source LLC
Chambersburg PA
CBHW021124300426
44113CB00006B/286